HIGHER

Program Authors

Nancy Frey

Lada Kratky

Nonie K. Lesaux

Sylvia Linan-Thompson

Deborah J. Short

Jennifer D. Turner

Australia · Brazil · Mexico · Singapore · United Kingdom · United States

National Geographic Learning,
a Cengage Company

Reach Higher 3B
Program Authors: Nancy Frey, Lada Kratky, Nonie K. Lesaux, Sylvia Linan-Thompson, Deborah J. Short, Jennifer D. Turner

Publisher, Content-based English:
Erik Gundersen

Associate Director, R&D: Barnaby Pelter

Senior Development Editors:
Jacqueline Eu
Ranjini Fonseka
Kelsey Zhang

Director of Global Marketing: Ian Martin

Heads of Regional Marketing:
Charlotte Ellis (Europe, Middle East and Africa)
Kiel Hamm (Asia)
Irina Pereyra (Latin America)

Product Marketing Manager: David Spain

Senior Production Controller: Tan Jin Hock

Senior Media Researcher (Covers): Leila Hishmeh

Senior Designer: Lisa Trager

Director, Operations: Jason Seigel

Operations Support:
Rebecca Barbush
Drew Robertson
Caroline Stephenson
Nicholas Yeaton

Manufacturing Planner: Mary Beth Hennebury

Publishing Consultancy and Composition:
MPS North America LLC

ISBN-13: 978-0-357-36689-9

National Geographic Learning
200 Pier Four Blvd
Boston, MA 02210
USA

Locate your local office at **international.cengage.com/region**

Visit National Geographic Learning online at **ELTNGL.com**
Visit our corporate website at **www.cengage.com**

Printed in China
Print Number: 09 Print Year: 2023

Contents at a Glance

Unit	Title	

5

6

7

8

Table of Contents

Mysteries of Matter

Unit 5

? BIG QUESTION

What causes matter to change?

Extra phonics support with **READ ON YOUR OWN**

Baby Birds Grow Up

We're All Going Places

Water Detective

SCIENCE

▸ Matter

Americans Today and Yesterday

Table of Contents

From Past to Present

Unit 6

? BIG QUESTION

How can we preserve our traditions?

Extra phonics support with **READ ON YOUR OWN**

Play It Safe

SOCIAL STUDIES

▸ Cultures and Traditions

Part 2

Stay Away! Come Here!

Table of Contents

Blast! Crash! Splash!

Unit 7

? BIG QUESTION

What forces can change Earth?

Extra phonics support with **READ ON YOUR OWN**

Puzzles and Maps

SCIENCE

▸ Forces of Nature

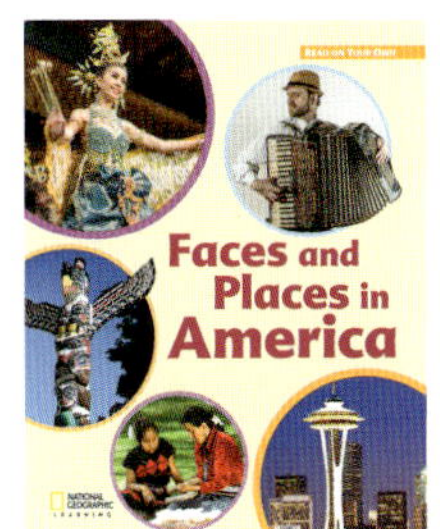

Faces and Places in America

Table of Contents

Getting There

Unit 8

BIG QUESTION

What tools can we use to achieve our goals?

Extra phonics support with **READ ON YOUR OWN**

A Nation Starts with Great People

MATH AND SOCIAL STUDIES

▸ Planning and Perseverance

Part 2

Water! Hot and Cool

Genres at a Glance

Fiction

Folk Tale

Historical Fiction

Legend and Myth

Realistic Fiction

Poetry

Narrative Poem

Song Lyrics

Drama

Play

Nonfiction

Biography/Profile

Descriptive Article

Human Interest Feature

Interview

Photo-Essay

Science Article

Media

E-Mail and Web-Based News Article

Online Article

Unit 5

Mysteries of Matter

What causes matter to change?

HERAT, AFGHANISTAN
An Afghan man crafting a glass object at his traditional glass shop

Unit at a Glance

- **Language Focus**: Describe Actions and Places
- **Reading Strategy**: Make Connections
- **Phonics Focus**: Endings: *-ed*, *-ing*; Prefixes: *in-*, *im-*
- **Topic**: Matter

Share What You Know

Do It!

1. **Put** one ice cube in a bowl on a table.
2. **Watch** what happens to the ice. How long did it take to melt?
3. **Draw** what you see. Describe your drawing to a partner.

PART 1 **Language Focus**

Language Frames

- When ______,
  I ______.
- When it is ______,
  I ______.

Describe Actions

Listen to Amita and David. Then use **Language Frames** to describe what you do in different kinds of weather.

When It Is Hot!

Dialogue 

1. When the weather is hot, I eat ice cream!

2. When it is cold, I eat ice cream, too.

3. You like ice cream when the weather is cold?

4. Yep! When it is cold, I can finish the ice cream before it melts!

5. When the weather is cold, I drink hot cocoa.

6. Me, too! It warms me up so I can eat more ice cream!

Science Vocabulary

Key Words
form
freeze
liquid
melt
solid
temperature
thermometer

Key Words

Look at the pictures. Use **Key Words** and other words to talk about **forms** of water.

Solid water **melts** when the **temperature** is warmer than 32°F.

Liquid water **freezes** when the temperature is 32°F or colder.

thermometer

32°F = 0°C

Talk Together

Tell a partner what causes water to change its form. Use **Key Words**. Then use **Language Frames** from page 4 to describe fun things you can do with water in different kinds of weather.

PART 1 Thinking Map

Character and Plot

When **characters** speak, you can find out:

- what the characters are like.
- what is happening in the **plot**.

Amita and David made up a skit about building a snowman. Look at the pictures and read the dialogue.

Map and Talk

You can make a chart that shows what characters say and what the words tell about the characters and the plot.

Character-Plot Chart

Character	What the Character Says	What This Shows About the Character	What This Shows About the Plot
Amita	"David builds the best snowmen!"	Amita values other people's work.	David is building a snowman.
David	"Thanks for your help, Amita!"	David accepts other people's help.	Amita is helping.

Talk Together

Plan and act out a short skit with a partner. Then use the characters' words to help you create a character-plot chart.

More Key Words

Use these words to talk about "Melt the Snow!" and "Saved in Ice."

alter

verb

When you **alter** something, you change it. She **alters** the dress to make it shorter.

occur

verb

When something **occurs**, it happens. A sunrise **occurs** every morning.

state

noun

The **state** of a person or thing is the way it is at a certain time. He is in a happy **state**.

substance

noun

Substance is the material that something is made of. Snow is a cold **substance**.

trap

verb

To **trap** something means to catch it and not let it go. Spiders **trap** insects with webs.

Talk Together

Work with a partner. Make a Word Web of examples for each **Key Word**.

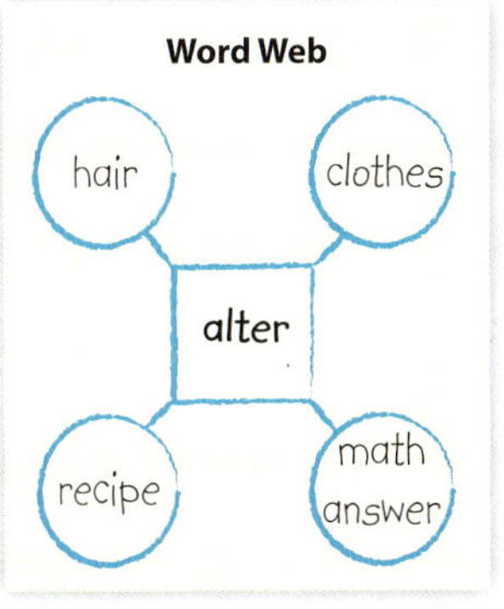

PART 1 **Reading Strategy**

Learn to Make Connections

Look at the picture. Does it make you think of something in your own life? **Make connections**, or compare what you see in the picture to your own experiences.

People feel better when the weather is warmer.

When you read, you **make connections**, too.

How to Make Connections

1. As you read, think about what is happening in the text.

2. Ask yourself, "What is this like in my own life?"

3. Think about how this connection helps you understand the text.

This is about ______.

I think of ______.

Now I understand ______.

Language Frames

This is about ______.

 I think of ______.

 Now I understand ______.

Talk Together

Read "A Change of Weather." Read the sample connection. Then use **Language Frames** to make connections. Tell a partner about them.

Story

A Change of Weather

Amita felt happy. It was her family's first picnic of the year. She didn't mind the slight chill in the air. Winter was over. It was spring!

Amita reached for a second piece of pie. Suddenly something touched her nose. She wiped it away. It was wet! Then it came again—and again! "Snowflakes!" she cried. She looked at the clouds. Their color had **altered** from gray to black. She shivered. It was suddenly much colder.

With a sigh, Mom packed up the picnic. Amita tried not to show it, but her happy **state** had vanished. Dad saw her disappointment.

"Quick changes in weather often **occur** in spring," he said gently. "Moisture in the air gets **trapped** in the clouds. When the **temperature** drops, the moisture turns to snow." He smiled and wiped a sticky **substance** off Amita's chin.

"Another snowflake?" she asked.

"Pie juice," Dad answered.

They both laughed.

Sample Connection

"This is about a picnic.

I think of picnics with my family. They are always lots of fun.

Now I understand why Amita feels happy."

PART 1 **Phonics Focus**

Endings: -ed, -ing

He kicked the ball.

He is kicking the ball.

Listen and Learn

Listen to each sentence. Choose the word that best finishes the sentence.

1. 

marched
marching
march
marches

The band is ______ in the parade.

2. 

picked
pick
picking
picks

We ______ some apples yesterday.

3. 

sprout
sprouted
sprouting
sprouts

The plant ______ two days ago.

4. 

stirred
stirs
stirring
stir

We are ______ the soup.

Talk Together

Listen and read. Find the words that end with *-ed* and *-ing*.

Over to You

Skating

When it gets cold enough, I can go skating. I look at the thermometer. It's telling me that the temperature is below freezing. The pond is frozen solid. Last night, it snowed, but today, the sun is shining. It's too cold for the sun to melt the snow. It's a good day for skating on the pond.

Out on the ice, my breath is forming little clouds in the air. My friends and I are chasing each other on the ice. We are turning this way and that way. We are racing on the ice. I wasn't interested in ice-skating last year. But then I learned how to skate. I couldn't wait for the pond to freeze. I love to skate now. When it is summer, I will go roller-skating.

Work with a partner.

Find and list the words that end with *-ed* and *-ing*. Then write these words without the endings.

Practice reading words with *-ed* and *-ing* endings by reading "Skating" with a partner.

Read a Play

Genre

A **play** is a story that is acted out on stage. In a play, actors pretend to be the characters. A written **script** tells the actors what to say and do.

Elements of Drama

The script for a play shows the **dialogue**, or the words the characters say. The **stage directions** tell the actors how to speak, look, and act.

stage directions

LITTLE ANT [*shaking with fear*]:

How scary! But don't worry, Mommy. I'll be very careful.

dialogue

[LITTLE ANT *bundles up and steps outside.*]

stage directions

Melt the Snow!

BY MARISA MONTES • ILLUSTRATED BY BRIAN AJHAR

Characters:

LITTLE ANT
MOMMY ANT

Outdoor Characters:

SNOW
SUN
CLOUD
WIND
WALL
MOUSE

CHORUS

▸ **Set a Purpose**

Find out why Little Ant's mother does not want her to play outside.

SCENE ONE

[LITTLE ANT ***peers*** *out the tiny window of her underground home. She sees* SUN *shining.*]

LITTLE ANT [*pointing*]**:** Look Mommy, the sun is shining. It's **melting** the snow. It's been such a long winter, and I'm tired of staying indoors. May I go out and play?

[MOMMY ANT *looks out the window. Outside,* WIND *begins to blow.* CLOUD ***appears in*** *the sky.*]

peers looks
appears in comes into

MOMMY ANT: But the wind is starting to blow, and dark clouds are forming. The air is chilly. It may snow again.

LITTLE ANT [***begging***]**:** Please, Mommy? ***Pretty please?*** I won't stay long.

MOMMY ANT [*sighing*]**:** OK, little one. But don't go far, and be very careful. If snow falls, you may get **trapped**. Then what would you do?

LITTLE ANT [*shaking with fear*]**:** How scary! But don't worry, Mommy. I'll be very careful.

[LITTLE ANT ***bundles up*** *and steps outside.*]

begging asking
Pretty, please? Will you please let me go?
bundles up puts on warm clothes

Before You Continue

1. **Drama** Find the dialogue that explains why Mommy Ant does not want Little Ant to play outside.
2. **Make Connections** Describe a time when you asked a parent to do something. How does this help you understand how Little Ant and Mommy Ant act?

Predict
What will happen to Little Ant when she plays outside?

SCENE TWO

[SUN *shines.* LITTLE ANT *skips happily in the forest. Suddenly,* WIND *blows.* CLOUD ***drifts*** *in front of* SUN. SNOW *falls.* LITTLE ANT ***shivers*** and stops. *A big snowflake lands on her leg and* ***traps*** *her. She* ***tugs*** *at her leg.*]

LITTLE ANT: Oh no! Snow, I'm stuck!
Give me back my leg so I can go home!

CHORUS: Snow holds Little Ant's leg,
And she wants to go home!

drifts moves slowly
shivers shakes from the cold
tugs pulls

SNOW: I'm sorry. I cannot. But there is someone stronger than me.

LITTLE ANT [*tugging at leg again*]**:** Who is stronger than you, heavy Snow?

SNOW: The sun is stronger. It **melts** me into water.

LITTLE ANT [*reaching toward* SUN]**:** Sun, melt the snow, *please!*

CHORUS: Sun, please melt Snow.
Snow holds Little Ant's leg,
And she wants to go home!

SUN: I cannot. But there is someone stronger than me.

LITTLE ANT [*looking* ***puzzled***]**:** Who is stronger than you, bright Sun?

SUN: It is the cloud. It covers my **warm rays**.

LITTLE ANT [*looking up at* CLOUD, *who is partly covering* SUN]**:** Cloud, please **uncover** the sun!

CHORUS: Cloud, please uncover Sun.
Sun must **melt** Snow.
Snow holds Little Ant's leg,
And she wants to go home!

puzzled confused
warm rays bright, warm light
uncover move away from

CLOUD: I am sorry. I cannot. But there is someone stronger than me.

LITTLE ANT [*shivering*]**:** Who is stronger than you, **thick** Cloud?

CLOUD: The wind is more powerful. It pushes me.

LITTLE ANT [***flinging*** *arms up and begging*]**:** Wind, push the cloud away, *please!*

CHORUS: Wind, please push Cloud,
So Cloud can uncover Sun,
So Sun can **melt** Snow.
Snow holds Little Ant's leg,
And she wants to go home!

thick big
flinging throwing

WIND: I'm sorry, Little Ant. I cannot help you. But there is someone stronger than me.

LITTLE ANT [*rubbing arms to warm up*]**:** Who could be stronger than you, **mighty** Wind?

WIND: It is the wall. **It holds me back.**

LITTLE ANT [***hanging head sadly*** *and shaking it slowly*]**:** *Oh dear!* [*turning to* WALL] Wall, do not hold back the wind, please!

mighty big, strong

It holds me back. I cannot blow through it.

hanging head sadly holding her head down in an unhappy way

block hold back; stop
amazed surprised

Before You Continue

1. **Confirm Prediction** Was your prediction about Little Ant correct? Explain.
2. **Cause/Effect** What effect does the wall have on Little Ant's situation?

Predict

Who will be strong enough to save Little Ant from her **trap**?

WALL: The mouse is stronger. He **gnaws** holes in me.

LITTLE ANT [*looking around quickly and seeing* MOUSE *near* WALL]**:** Mouse, please gnaw at Wall so I can go home!

gnaws chews

CHORUS: Mouse, please gnaw at Wall,
So Wall will not block Wind,
For Wind must push Cloud,
So Cloud can uncover Sun,
So Sun can **melt** Snow.
Snow holds Little Ant's leg,
And she wants to go home!

[MOUSE ***scampers*** *to* LITTLE ANT]

MOUSE: I will help you—of course! We tiny **creatures** must **stick together** against those stronger than us. It will be a tasty treat! Yum yum! [*showing teeth*]

scampers runs
creatures animals
stick together help each other

CHORUS: Mouse, gnaw at Wall!
Wall, stop blocking Wind!
Wind, push Cloud!
Cloud, uncover Sun!
Sun, **melt** the snow!
Snow is holding Little Ant's leg,
And she wants to go home!

[MOUSE *gnaws at* WALL. WALL ***crumbles*** *and stops blocking* WIND. WIND *blows over* WALL *and pushes* CLOUD. CLOUD ***glides*** *away from* SUN. SUN **melts** SNOW.]

[LITTLE ANT *shakes her leg loose.*]

LITTLE ANT: I'm free! I can go home! [***hooks elbows*** *with* MOUSE *and dances*] Thank you, thank you my friend, for saving me! You are the strongest one of all!

crumbles breaks into pieces
glides moves smoothly
hooks elbows joins arms

SCENE THREE

[LITTLE ANT *bursts through the kitchen door of her home.*]

LITTLE ANT: Mommy, Mommy! I'm back!

MOMMY ANT [*running toward the door and* **scooping** *up* LITTLE ANT *in her arms*]**:** You're just in time, little one.

LITTLE ANT [*jumping excitedly*]**:** In time for what, Mommy?

MOMMY ANT: I made a pot of hot chocolate, **rich** and sweet! Are you cold? ❖

scooping picking
rich strong

Before You Continue

1. **Confirm Prediction** Who is the strongest character? Are you surprised?
2. **Drama** Read the stage directions on page 25. How do the characters work together to free Little Ant?

Meet the Author

Marisa Montes

Marisa Montes was born in Puerto Rico, but she lived in California. Growing up, she spoke Spanish at home and English at school. As a young girl, she lived in France and spoke French with her neighborhood friends.

Like Little Ant, Montes loved to be outdoors. "I can't stand the feeling that there is something out there that I might be missing out on." Montes loved animals, so she often included them in her stories.

Writing Tip

Marisa Montes used vivid words to describe the power of each character in the play. Write a sentence to describe your favorite character. Use vivid words in your description.

PART 1 **Think and Respond**

Key Words

alter	solid
form	state
freeze	substance
liquid	temperature
melt	thermometer
occur	trap

Talk About It

1. Suppose you are going to perform in the **play**. How will the **dialogue** and **stage directions** help you?

   The dialogue tells me ____. The stage directions tell me ____.

2. Think of the beginning of the play. **Describe** the **actions** of Little Ant and Mommy Ant.

   Little Ant ____. Mommy Ant ____.

3. Think about the character of Mouse. Why does he help Little Ant? What does this show about him?

   Mouse helps Little Ant because ____.
   This shows that he ____.

Write About It

At the end of the play, Mommy Ant says, "Are you cold?" What do you think Little Ant will say? Write a line or two of dialogue for Little Ant to answer Mommy Ant's question. Use at least one **Key Word**.

LITTLE ANT: Yes/No, ____.

Character and Plot

Create a character-plot chart for "Melt the Snow!" Write dialogue that you think is important.

Character-Plot Chart

Character	What the Character Says	What This Shows About the Character	What This Shows About the Plot
Mommy Ant	"Don't go far, and be very careful."	Mommy Ant wants Little Ant to be safe.	Mommy Ant lets Little Ant go out to play.
Little Ant			

Discuss your chart with a partner. Take turns reading what the characters say. Explain how the dialogue helps you understand the characters and the plot. Use the sentence frame and **Key Words**.

This dialogue shows that ____.

Fluency

Practice reading with expression. Rate your reading.

Talk Together

What caused the snow to **melt**? Draw a picture to show how Little Ant got free. Share your picture with the class. Use **Key Words** to describe the picture.

Antonyms

Antonyms are words that have opposite meanings. Look at each pair of antonyms below. Compare the two words.

freeze

melt

freeze: to turn a liquid substance into a solid one

melt: to turn a solid substance into a liquid one

trap

free

trap: to hold a person or animal against its will

free: to let a person or animal go

Try It Together

Read the sentences. Then answer the questions below.

Think of the water you drink. That's liquid water. Think of a glacier. That's solid water. If a glacier starts to melt, is the temperature hot or cold?

1. What is an antonym for liquid?

- **A** cold
- **B** melt
- **C** solid
- **D** water

2. What is an antonym for cold?

- **A** hot
- **B** liquid
- **C** freeze
- **D** temperature

Making Connections Read about another animal that got **trapped** when water changed to ice.

Genre An **e-mail** is an electronic message. A **web-based news article** is a story on the Internet about something important or interesting.

SAVED IN ICE

Frozen Baby Mammoth Found

Before You Continue

1. **Predict** Based on the title, what do you think this selection is about?
2. **Make Connections** Look at the photo. Does the baby mammoth look familiar to you? Explain.

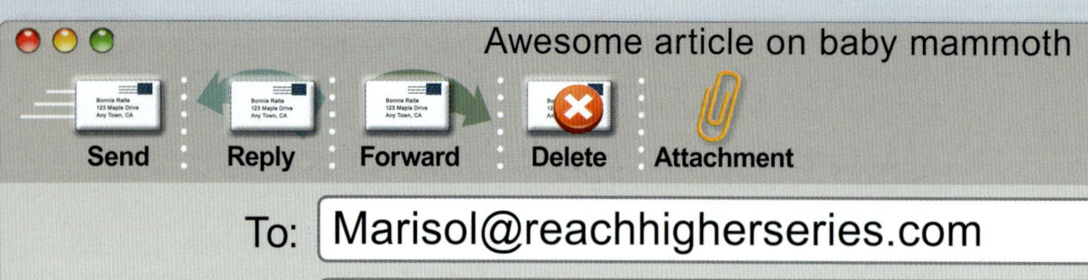

To: Marisol@reachhigherseries.com

From: Rudy@reachhigherseries.com

Subject: Awesome article on baby mammoth

Attachment:

Hey Marisol!

Check out this **awesome** article! It's about a baby **mammoth** that's been frozen in ice for 40,000 years!

Here's the link to the article:
https://eltngl.com/reachhigherseries

I know how much you love elephants. So I thought you'd think this was really cool!

See you at school tomorrow!

Rudy

awesome amazing
mammoth elephant-like animal

Photo in the News: Baby Mammoth Found Frozen in Russia

https://eltngl.com/reachhigherseries

HOME • FEATURES • FOLLOW UP • KIDS • BLOG • RESOURCES

NEWS ARTICLE | Photo Gallery | Related Articles | Maps | Search

Photo in the News: Baby Mammoth Found Frozen in Russia

by **Christine Dell'Amore**

July 11, 2007— Talk about a **mammoth** surprise.

In May 2007, a hunter was walking in the Yamalo-Nenetsk region, in the far north of Russia. Suddenly, he saw something sticking out of the damp snow. He thought it was a frozen **reindeer**. When the hunter looked closer, he realized that it was something else. The "reindeer" was really a 40,000-year-old baby mammoth. It was **perfectly preserved** in ice.

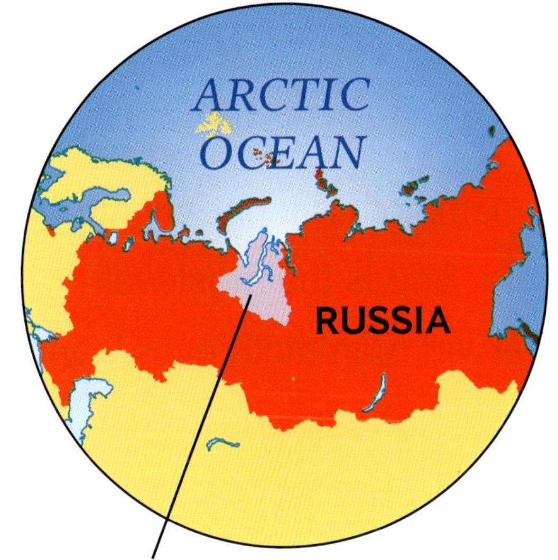

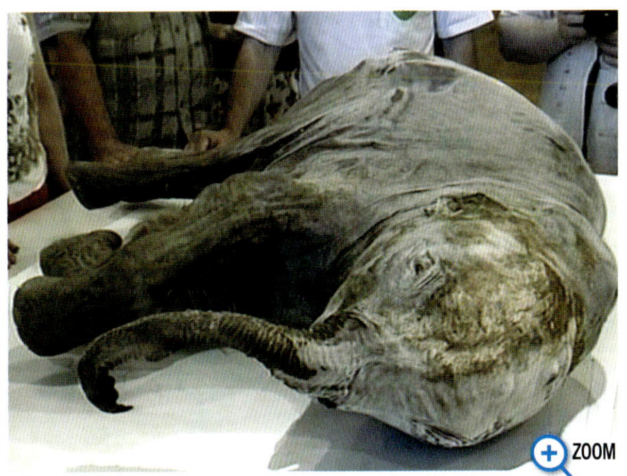

▲ The last mammoths died long ago, but they are related to the elephants that live today in Africa and Asia.

NEXT ››

mammoth huge
reindeer kind of deer that lives in very cold places
perfectly preserved completely saved

Before You Continue

1. **Media** Where does Rudy find the article about the mammoth? How does he send it?
2. **Draw Conclusions** Where did some mammoths live 40,000 years ago?

Photo in the News: Baby Mammoth Found Frozen in Russia

https://eltngl.com/reachhigherseries

HOME • FEATURES • FOLLOW UP • KIDS • BLOG • RESOURCES

NEWS ARTICLE | Photo Gallery | Related Articles | Maps | Search

Frozen in Ice: Baby Mammoth Found Frozen in Russia

Lovely Lyuba

The mammoth is a one-month-old female. She is the most well-preserved mammoth ever found. Mammoths have not lived on Earth since the last **Ice Age**. That was 11,500 to 1.8 million years ago.

"It's a lovely little baby mammoth," says a Russian scientist. "She **was found in perfect condition**."

The baby mammoth weighs 110 pounds and **measures 51 inches**. She is the size of a large dog, reporters say.

▲ Hair is still attached to the mammoth's leg.

Ice Age time when ice covered much of Earth

was found in perfect condition looks like she did when she was alive

measures 51 inches is 51 inches long

▲ A boy touches Lyuba in a museum in Russia.

The female mammoth was named “Lyuba” after the Russian hunter’s wife. Scientists believe Lyuba will help them discover some of the secrets of these animals from long ago.

Lyuba **has recently gone on display**. Now people can share in the discovery by seeing her for themselves. ❖

▲ Lyuba on display in Tokyo

« PREVIOUS

has recently gone on display can now be seen in a museum

Before You Continue

1. **Details** How old was the mammoth when she was **trapped** in ice?
2. **Make Connections** The mammoth is the size of a large dog. How does this help you understand more about her?

PART 1 **Respond and Extend**

Key Words

alter	solid
form	state
freeze	substance
liquid	temperature
melt	thermometer
occur	trap

Compare Media

Rudy's e-mail and the online article, "Saved in Ice," are both electronic **forms** of communication. In what other ways are the forms the same? How are they different?

Work with a partner to complete the comparison chart. Write *yes* or *no* for each feature.

Comparison Chart

	Rudy's E-mail	"Saved in Ice"
electronic form of communication	yes	yes
formal language		
informal language		
personal information		
factual information		

Talk Together

In the e-mail and the article, you read about a 40,000-year-old baby mammoth. Why was the mammoth **trapped**? Think about what causes water to change its form. Use **Key Words** to talk about your ideas.

Adjectives and Articles

An **adjective** tells about a noun. An **article** points to a noun.

Grammar Rules Adjectives and Articles

• Use **adjectives** to tell what something is like.	The **bright** sun shines. The sky is **blue**.
• For most adjectives, add -**er** to compare two things. Add -**est** to compare three or more things.	My horn is small**er** than your horn. His horn is the small**est** one of all.
• Use **this** or **that** to tell "which one."	**This** horn is old. Is **that** horn new?
• Use **articles** to identify a **noun**.	**An** **ant** looks at **the** **sun** through **a** **window**.

Read Adjectives and Articles

Read these sentences about "Melt the Snow!" Find two articles and three different kinds of adjectives. Show them to a partner.

> Heavy snow falls in the forest. A snowflake falls on Little Ant's leg! Sun is stronger than Snow. Can Sun melt that snowflake?

Write Adjectives and Articles

Write two sentences about the weather. Use at least one adjective and one article. Read your sentences to a partner.

PART 2 Language Focus

Describe Places

Listen to Marita's chant. Then use **Language Frames** to describe a place you know.

Language Frames

- Here is ______.
- The ______ is ______.
- It feels ______.

At the Beach

Chant 

Here is a beach, a sunny beach.
I cannot wait for a swim.
The sand is hot and dry from the sun.
It feels gritty on my skin.

Here is the water, the chilly water.
The gentle waves are a treat.
The sand is wet and soft from the waves.
It feels squishy under my feet.

wave

Science Vocabulary

Key Words
ground
mixture
sand
water
wetland

Key Words

Look at this picture. Use **Key Words** and other words to talk about how a **wetland** can form.

How a Wetland Forms

Talk Together

What causes water and sand to change into a wetland? Use **Key Words** to explain. Then use **Language Frames** from page 38 to describe a wetland.

Cause and Effect

Most events have a **cause** and an **effect**.

- To figure out an effect, ask, "What happened?"
- To figure out a cause, ask, "Why did it happen?"

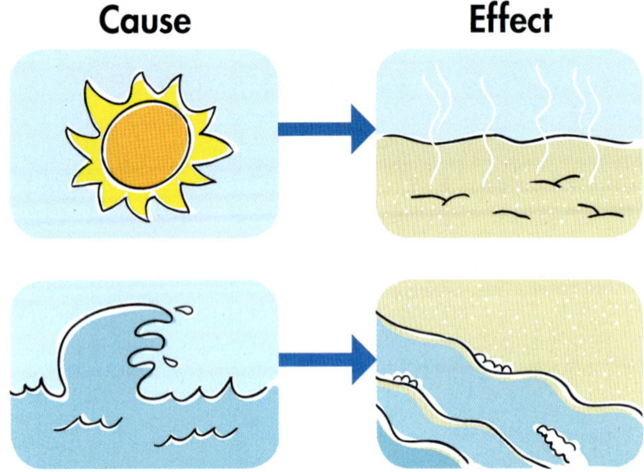

Map and Talk

You can use a chart to show causes and effects. To make the chart, write an event in column 1. In column 2, write what happened because of the event.

Cause-and-Effect Chart

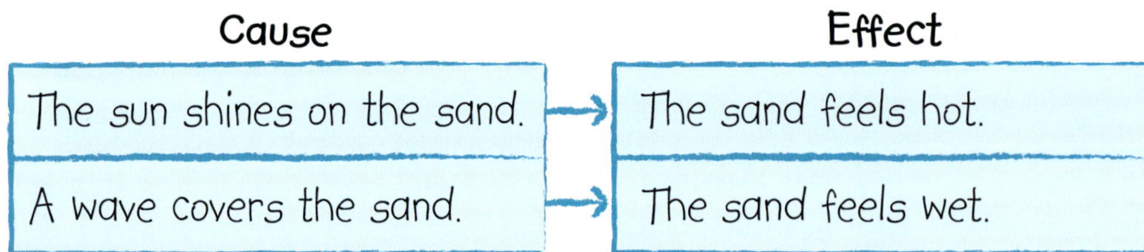

Cause	Effect
The sun shines on the sand.	The sand feels hot.
A wave covers the sand.	The sand feels wet.

Talk Together

Tell a partner about something that happened. Then work together to make a cause-and-effect chart for the event.

More Key Words

Use these words to talk about "Quicksand: When Earth Turns to Liquid" and "Meet Maycira Costa."

area
noun

An **area** is a part of a place. A classroom can have an **area** for reading.

combine
verb

When you **combine** things, you mix them together. What foods does she **combine**?

composition
noun

Composition is what things are made of. The **composition** of mud is dirt and water.

firm
adjective

Something that is **firm** is hard. You can skate on ice because it is **firm**.

surface
noun

A **surface** is the outside part of something. The **surface** of this ball is bumpy.

Talk Together

Make a Word Map for each **Key Word**. Then compare your maps with a partner's.

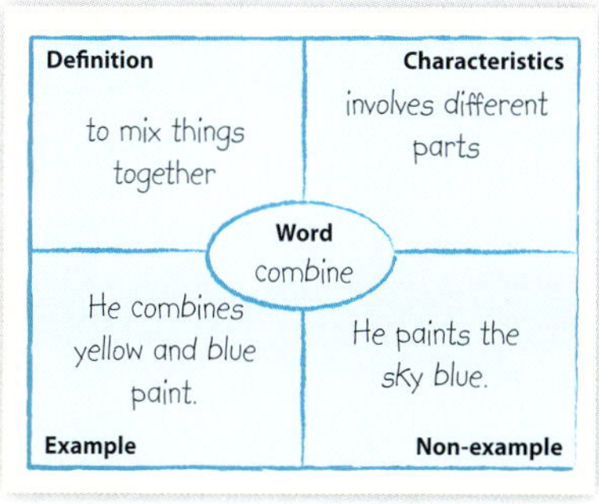

PART 2 **Reading Strategy**

Learn to Make Connections

Look at the photograph. Does it make you think of something you have read or something you know about? This is called **making connections**.

When you read, you can understand more if you **make connections**.

How to Make Connections

1. Think about what the text is about.
2. As you read, think about other things you have read or an issue that you know about. Does the text relate to these?
3. Decide how the connection helps you understand the text.

The topic is ______.

This makes me think of ______.

Now I understand ______.

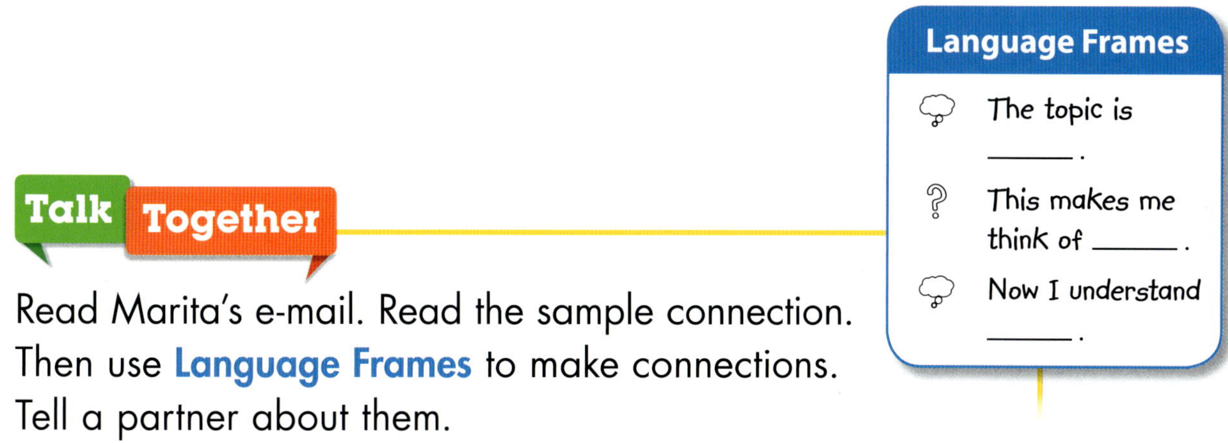

Talk Together

Read Marita's e-mail. Read the sample connection. Then use **Language Frames** to make connections. Tell a partner about them.

Language Frames

- The topic is ______.
- This makes me think of ______.
- Now I understand ______.

E-Mail

Send Forward Delete

To: Anna@reachhigherseries.com

From: Marita@reachhigherseries.com

Subject: My Boat Ride on the Marsh

Attachment:

Dear Anna,

Yesterday I took a boat ride on a marsh. The whole **area** is home to thousands of wild birds. The ride started well. But then I stood up to take a picture of a wild duck when—you won't believe this—I FELL OUT OF THE BOAT!

Thank goodness, the **water** was shallow, but the **ground** under my feet felt squishy. I couldn't find a **firm** place to stand!

The water was salty, too. It tasted AWFUL. The guide pulled me back into the boat. Then she explained the **composition** of the water. "Tidewater from the sea **combines** with freshwater flowing out to the sea," she said. "That makes the water salty."

Well, it made me gag! Not only that, the **surface** of the water was covered with green algae. GROSS! The marsh was interesting, but I never planned to take it home!

Marita

Sample Connection

"The topic is a boat ride on a marsh. This makes me think of a picture I saw of a marsh. Now I understand why Marita rode in a boat."

◀ = A good place to make a connection

PART 2 Phonics Focus

Prefixes: *in-*, *im-*

incomplete = not complete

impossible = not possible

Listen and Learn

Listen to the words and definitions. Match each word to the correct definition.

1. imperfect	not polite
2. incorrect	not active
3. indirect	not perfect
4. impolite	not proper
5. improper	not direct
6. inactive	not correct

Choose two words from the list above. Write your own sentences using the words.

Talk Together

Listen and read. Find the words with the prefixes *in-* and *im-*.

Over to You

Wetlands

Wetlands lie between dry land and water. They contain a lot of water. They can have salt water. They can have fresh water. They can have a mixture of both. The ground in a wetland feels soft.

Some people think a wetland is an imperfect place. That is incorrect. Wetlands do many things. Wetlands filter impure water. They help keep rivers at the right level. Wetlands protect the land from floods. They are home to many animals. It would be impossible to have a healthy environment without wetlands.

Work with a partner.

Point to a word with the prefix *in-* or *im-* and have your partner say it. Then take turns using the words in oral sentences.

Practice reading words with prefixes by reading "Wetlands" with a partner.

Read a Science Article

Genre

A **science article** is nonfiction. It can tell how something in nature works.

Text Feature

A **diagram** is a drawing that shows where things are, how something works, or when something happens. It has **captions**, or **labels**, that tell more about the drawing.

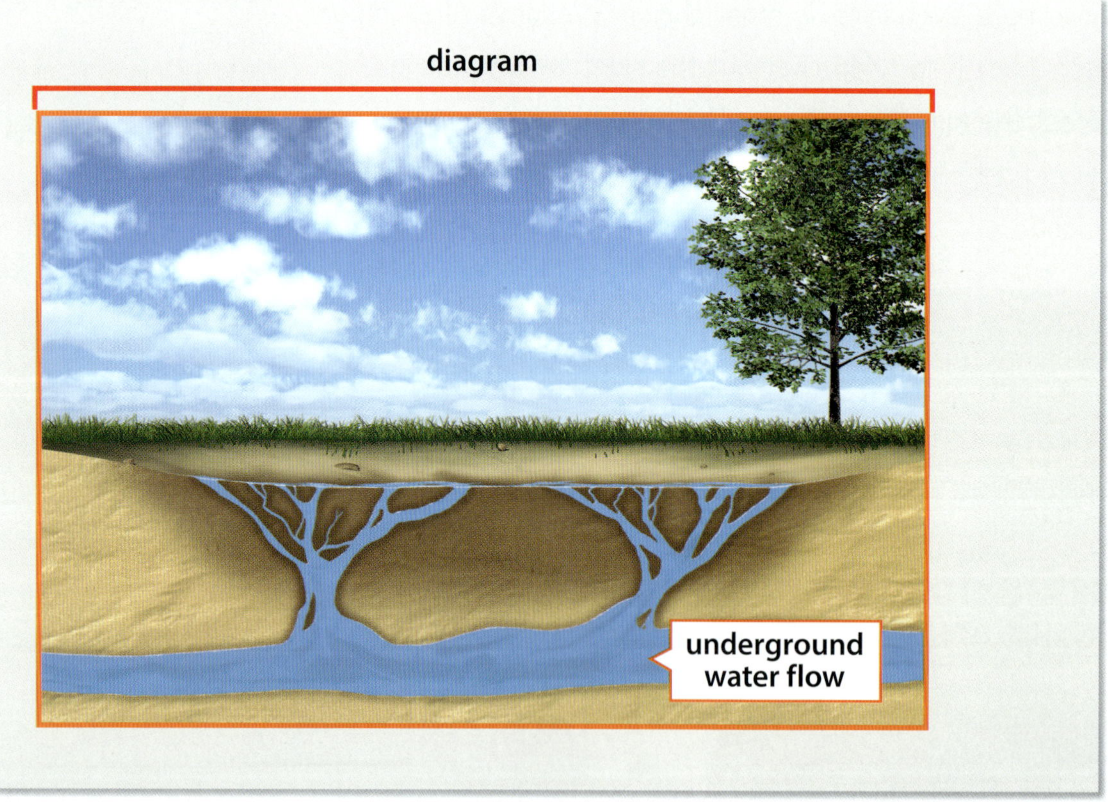

Quicksand:

When Earth Turns to Liquid

by Kris Hirschmann

▸ **Set a Purpose**
Find out if quicksand is really as dangerous as it seems.

What Is Quicksand?

The word *quicksand* makes some people **shiver with fear**. This is probably because of the way many movies show quicksand. In films, quicksand is often **a mysterious substance** that sucks people and animals to their deaths!

Movies do not always show the truth about quicksand.

shiver with fear feel very afraid
a mysterious substance something that cannot be explained

Actual quicksand is very different from movie quicksand. It **rarely harms** people or animals. Real quicksand is not mysterious. It is a simple substance that forms naturally.

Quicksand is often just **sand** with a lot of **water** between its **particles**. This makes the sand soupy, or runny. When the **waterlogged** sand can no longer **support** weight, it is called "quick."

Quicksand is not very hard to find. It is often just a mixture of water and sand. ▶

rarely harms usually doesn't hurt
particles tiny pieces
waterlogged very wet
support hold up

Before You Continue

1. **Make Connections** Have you ever walked in sand or on sandy ground? Compare how that felt with the way quicksand is described on this page.
2. **Cause/Effect** What happens when a lot of water mixes with sand?

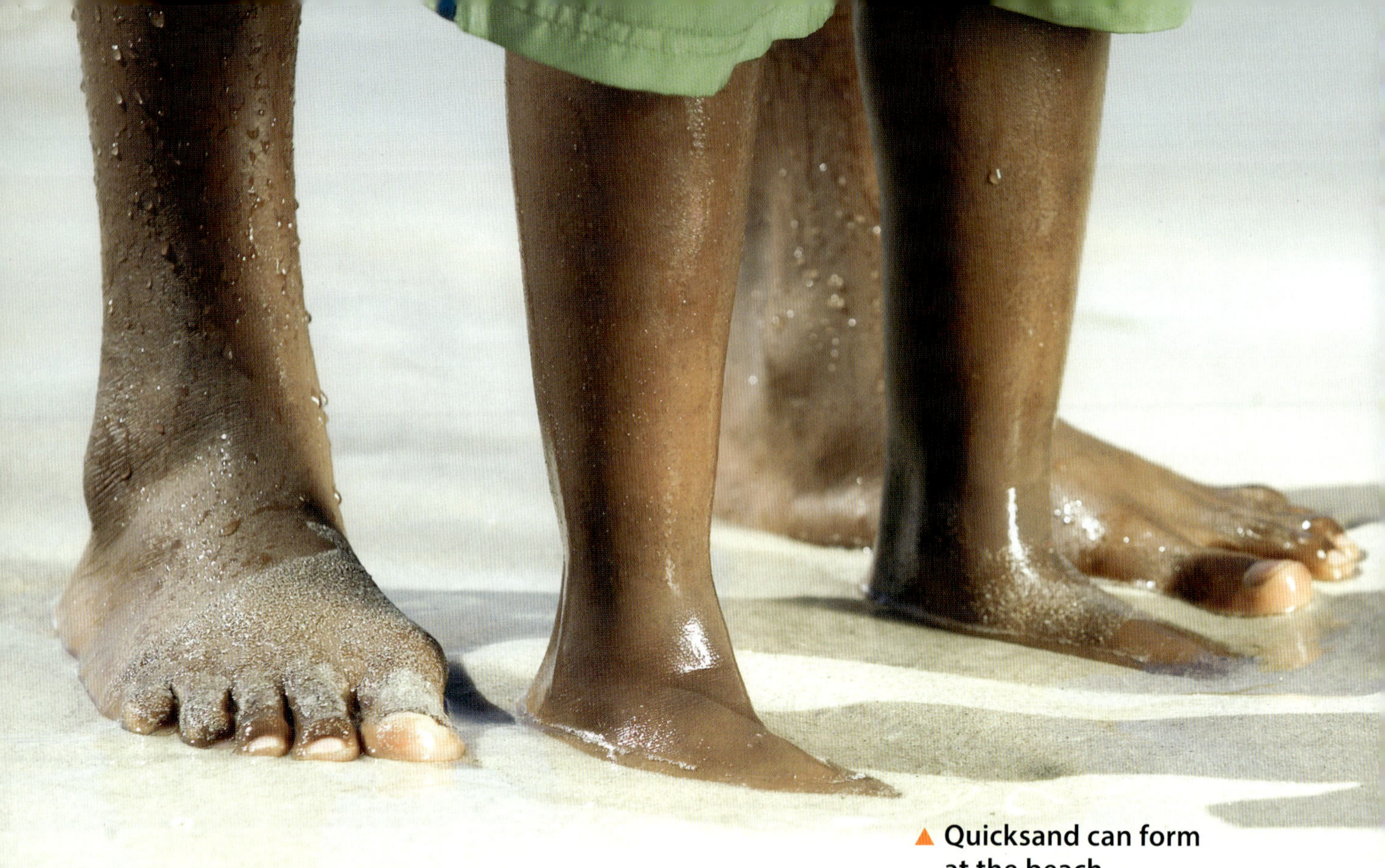

▲ Quicksand can form at the beach.

Sand and Other Materials

A beach is a good place to see how **water** **affects** **sand**. In the **area** where waves roll onto the land, the sand changes. Here, water sinks into the sand. The water makes the sand loose and soft. For a few seconds, the **surface** acts like **shallow quicksand**.

Materials Things in Nature
affects can make a change in
shallow quicksand quicksand that is not deep

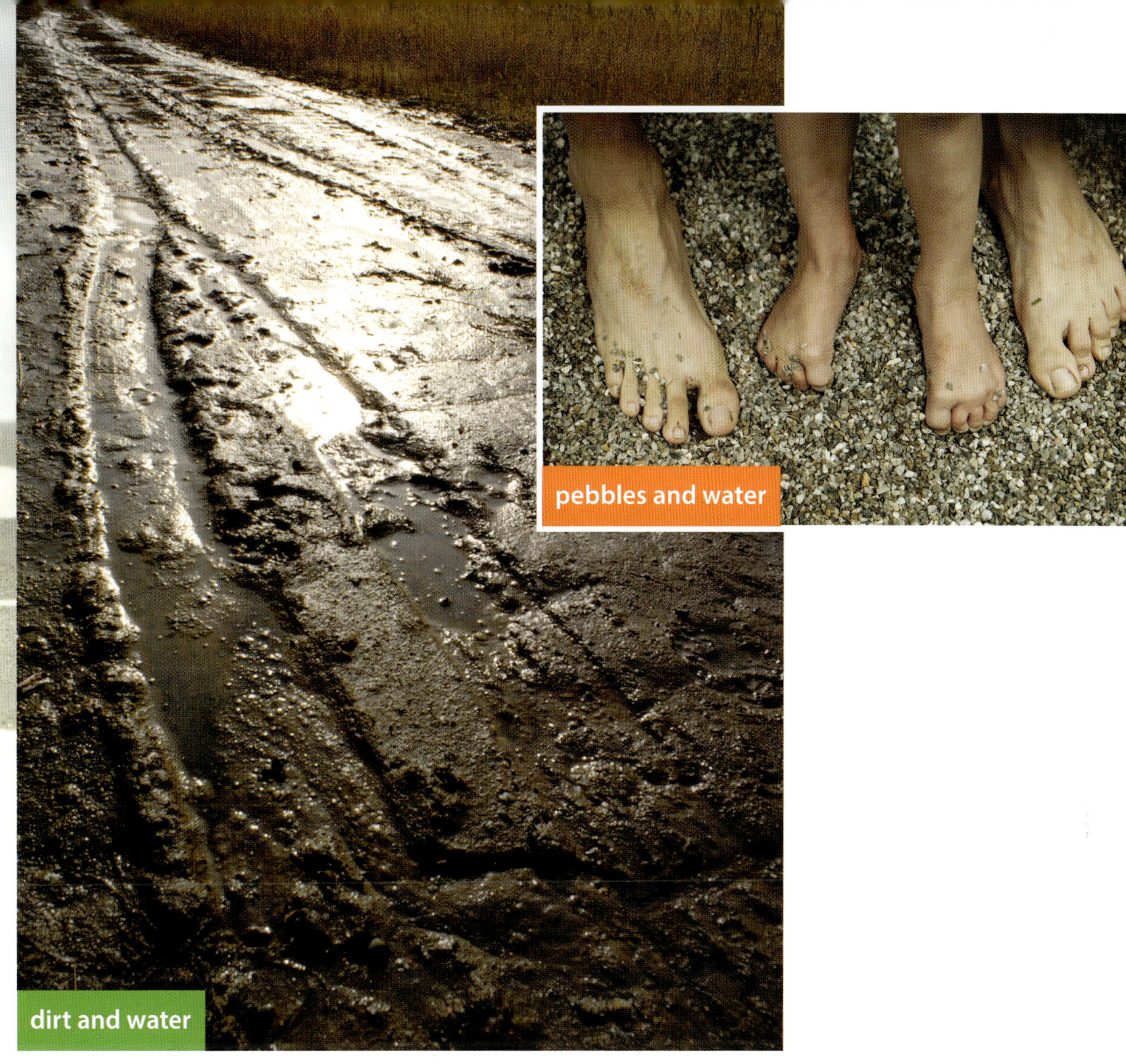
pebbles and water

dirt and water

Sand is not the only substance that can become quick. Dirt, pebbles, and gravel can also **quicken** under the right conditions. This means that sometimes **water** mixes with one of these materials in just the right way. Then quicksand forms.

quicken become quicksand

Before You Continue

1. **Cause/Effect** How do waves affect the **sand** on a beach?
2. **Details** What other materials can **combine** with **water** to quicken?

How Does Quicksand Form?

Most of the time, particles of **sand**, dirt, and pebbles are packed close together to form a solid, **stable** **ground**. **Firm** ground can support the weight of a person, a car, or even a building.

Solid ground is firm enough to hold up this car.

stable strong, unmoving

How Quicksand Forms

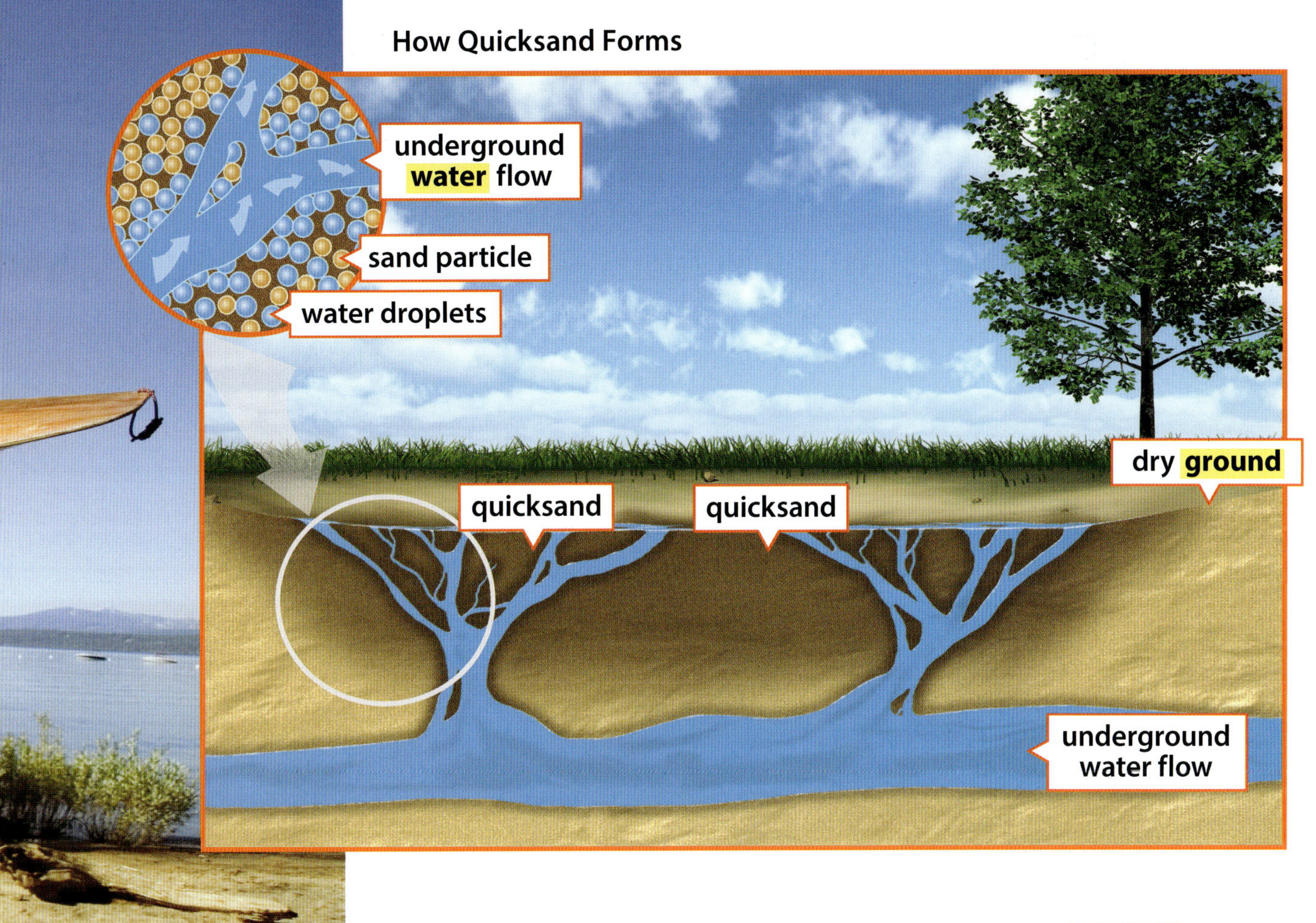

Conditions change when underground **water** forces its way between particles. The water pushes the particles farther apart. The solid **ground starts to act like a liquid**. It is now quicksand. As long as the water **flows**, the particles will stay in their liquid state.

starts to act like a liquid becomes thin and watery

flows keeps moving

Before You Continue

1. **Cause/Effect** Why does solid ground support heavy weights?
2. **Use Text Features** Use the diagram to tell a partner how quicksand forms.

Where Is Quicksand Found?

Water is the **key ingredient in** quicksand. This means that quicksand is usually found in **wetlands**, or watery places. Marshes, rivers, creeks, and swamps often hide pools of quicksand.

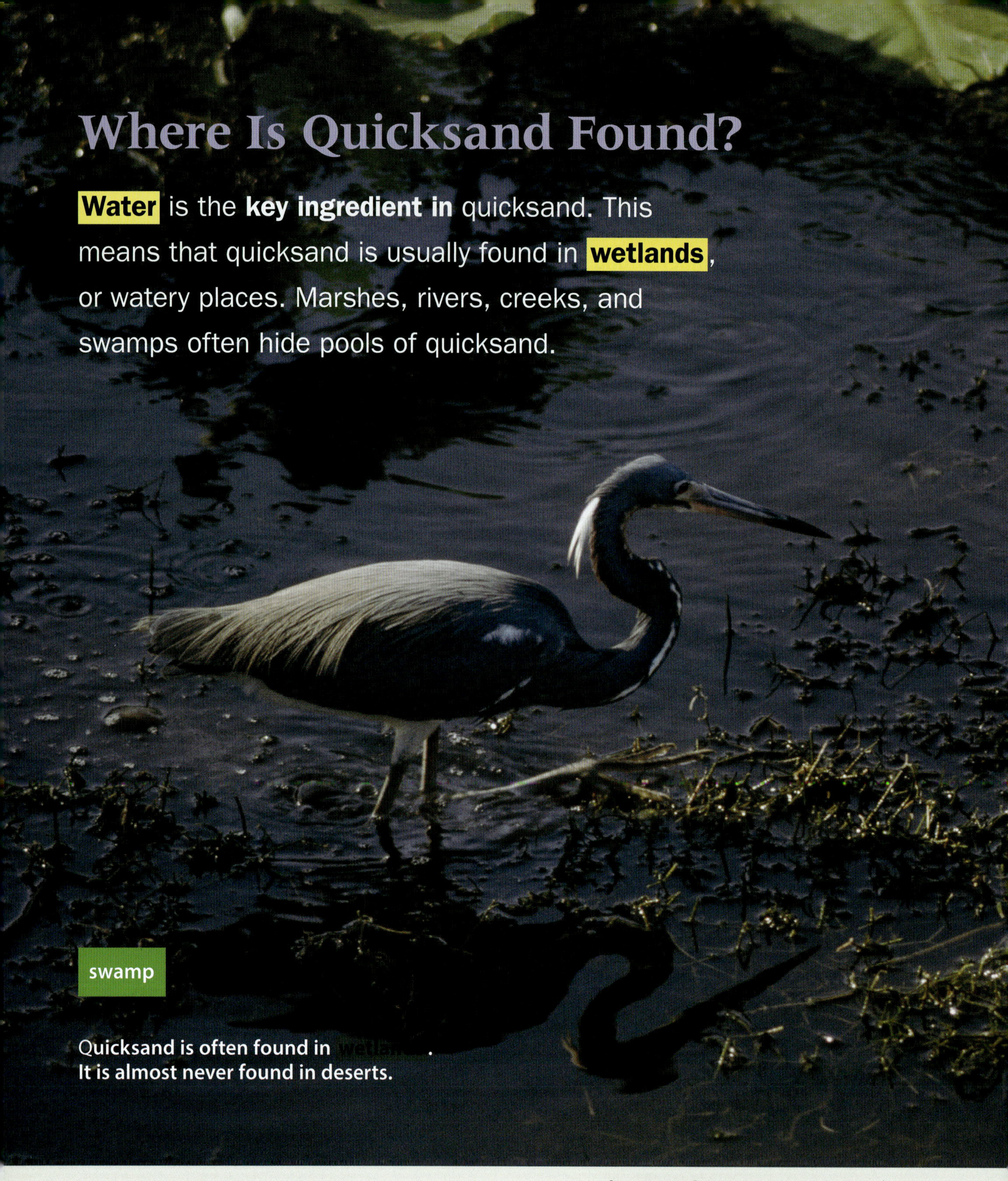

Quicksand is often found in wetlands. It is almost never found in deserts.

key ingredient in most important part of

Deserts have a lot of **sand**, but they almost never **contain** quicksand. Deserts are dry places. Quicksand usually will not form without **water**. It does not matter how much sand there is in a place!

desert

Think about movie quicksand again. Is quicksand really a mysterious substance? Does it really suck people and animals to their deaths? Now that you know the truth, you might not be so scared the next time you see quicksand in a movie! ❖

contain have

Before You Continue

1. **Cause/Effect** Why do deserts rarely have quicksand?
2. **Make Connections** Have you ever seen quicksand? How do you know it is quicksand? Use details from the text to explain your answer.

Quicksand Myths

Fiction	Fact
Quicksand sucks you down. 	Quicksand is thicker than **water**. It is easier for things to float in quicksand than in water. It is almost impossible to sink under completely. 
Quicksand is alive. 	Quicksand is not alive. When a person steps into quicksand, it moves **with the person's motion**. Quicksand only looks like it is alive. 

Quicksand Myths false things people believe about quicksand

Fiction things that are not true

Fact things that are true

with the person's motion when the person moves

More Quicksand Myths

Fiction	Fact
Leeches and worms live in quicksand.	There is rarely anything alive in quicksand. So don't worry about leeches or worms.

Fiction	Fact
Quicksand **is bottomless**.	There are places with very deep quicksand. However, quicksand is not bottomless. Most quicksand is a few inches deep to less than waist-deep.

Leeches Worms that suck blood
is bottomless goes down forever

Before You Continue

1. **Draw Conclusions** Should you be afraid to walk in quicksand? Explain.
2. **Explain** Choose a myth about quicksand from the article. What is fiction about the myth? What is fact?

PART 2 Think and Respond

Key Words	
area	mixture
combine	sand
composition	surface
firm	water
ground	wetland

Talk About It

1. Tell one fact you learned in the **science article** about quicksand.

   I learned _____.

2. Quicksand usually forms in **areas** with a lot of **water**. Use the photos in the article to **describe** a **place** like this.

   A place with quicksand often looks _____.

3. In your own words, tell how quicksand forms.

   Quicksand forms when _____.

Write About It

There are a lot of myths about quicksand. What did you believe about quicksand before you read the article? Write a paragraph. Tell what you believed and whether or not it is true. Use **Key Words** if you can.

Before I read the article, I thought _____.
As I read, I learned _____.

Reread and Summarize

Cause and Effect

Complete a cause-and-effect chart for "Quicksand: When Earth Turns to Liquid."

Cause-and-Effect Chart

With a partner, use your chart to summarize the causes and effects of quicksand. Ask the questions in the speech balloon and use **Key Words**. Record your summary.

What happened?
Why did it happen?

Fluency

Practice reading with intonation. Rate your reading.

Talk Together

What causes matter to change? Make two pictures to show how **water** can cause quicksand. Use **Key Words** as labels. Share your pictures with the class.

PART 2 Word Work

Synonyms

Synonyms are words that have almost the same meaning.

Mixture and **blend** are synonyms. Read the caption for the picture. How are the meanings of the two words alike?

Concrete is a blend of many materials. It is a mixture of lime, cement, water, sand, and tiny pieces of rock.

Try It Together

Read the passage. Then answer the questions.

At the beach, quicksand is usually in an area close to the water. If you stand in this place for a few seconds, your feet might sink into the soft sand. If you want to stand on a firm surface, you need to climb on some hard rocks!

1. What is a synonym for area?

- **A** sand
- **B** place
- **C** water
- **D** stand

2. What is a synonym for firm?

- **A** soft
- **B** hard
- **C** rocks
- **D** surface

Making Connections Read an interview with a scientist to find out more about **wetlands**.

Genre During an **interview**, one person asks another person questions to get information. The results of the interview are often shared in a question-and-answer format.

Meet Maycira Costa

by Nora Brook

▲ Dr. Maycira Costa

Squish, splash, slosh!

That's the sound of feet walking through a **wetland**. To Dr. Maycira Costa, that sound is like music. Dr. Costa studies wetlands. Find out why she loves these **soggy** spaces.

soggy wet and soft

▸ Before You Continue

1. **Visualize** Describe what it feels and sounds like to walk over wet, soggy land.
2. **Make Inferences** Why does the author say that sounds of the wetlands are like music to Dr. Costa?

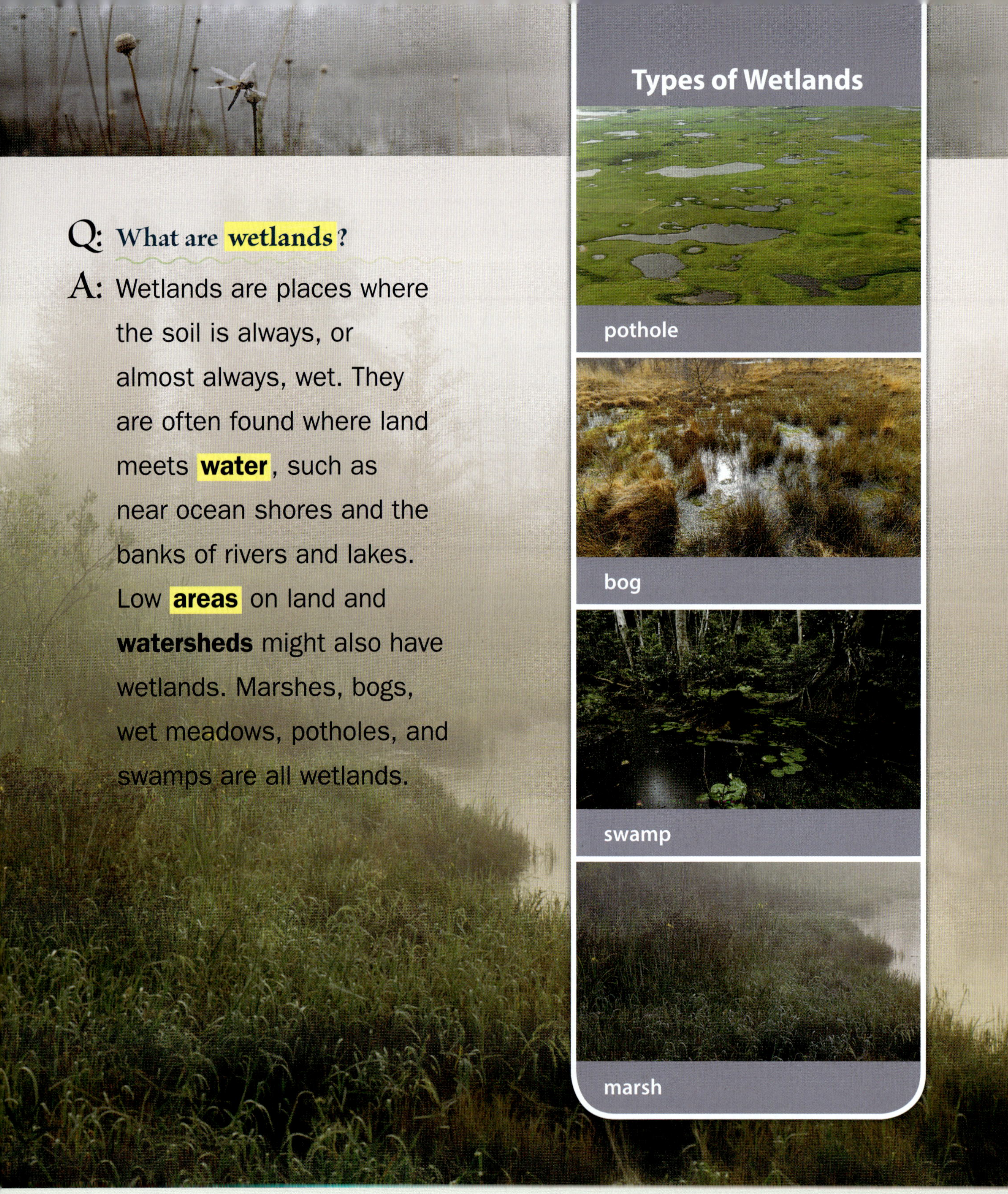

Q: What are wetlands?

A: Wetlands are places where the soil is always, or almost always, wet. They are often found where land meets **water**, such as near ocean shores and the banks of rivers and lakes. Low **areas** on land and **watersheds** might also have wetlands. Marshes, bogs, wet meadows, potholes, and swamps are all wetlands.

Types of Wetlands

pothole

bog

swamp

marsh

watersheds places that hold **water**

Q: What makes wetlands special? Why do you study them?

A: Wetland ecosystems are very important. They are a **habitat** for many kinds of plants and animals. They help control floods. They can even filter, or clean, water. I want to learn how **climate changes** and human activities, like farming, affect wetlands. I hope my work helps people understand wetlands and **value** them.

Animals In the Wetlands

tapir

caiman

egret

jaguar

habitat home
climate changes changes in weather
value take care of

Before You Continue

1. **Cause/Effect** What kinds of things could affect wetlands? Use details from the text to name them.
2. **Make Connections** Think of a time you saw a wetland, in images or in real life. How do your ideas about them compare with Dr. Costa's ideas? Explain.

Q: Where are the wetlands you study?

A: I study the Pantanal and Amazon wetlands in South America. They are the largest **tropical** wetlands in the world. The Pantanal alone is almost as big as the state of New York!

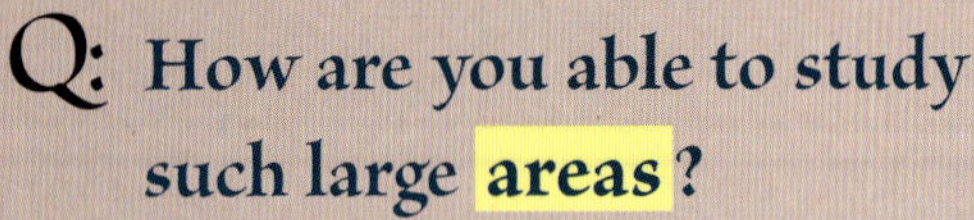

Q: How are you able to study such large areas?

A: I look at images taken from satellites orbiting high above Earth. They show where the water is, and how much sand, dirt, and other **sediment** is in it. I also **go into the field** and take samples.

satellite image of Brazil

Dr. Costa with her son at a lake in Brazil

tropical hot and steamy

sediment matter that settles to the bottom of a liquid

go into the field walk into a wetland

Q: When you are in the field, do you ever worry about things like quicksand?

A: No! Humans are not as **dense** as quicksand, so we easily float in it. If you step in quicksand, do not panic. You will not sink!

Q: What advice do you have for young explorers?

A: Be curious about nature. Do not be afraid. No matter where you live, there is probably a **wetland** nearby. Gather your friends and family and go explore it! ❖

Students explore a wetland.

dense heavy

Before You Continue

1. **Make Connections** What does Dr. Costa say about quicksand? Does this remind you of another selection you've read? Explain.
2. **Generalize** How does technology developed for space exploration affect Dr. Costa's research on **wetlands**?

PART 2 **Respond and Extend**

Key Words

area	mixture
combine	sand
composition	surface
firm	water
ground	wetland

Compare Text Features

Study the Venn diagram with a partner. Then use the text features below to complete the diagram.

chart	diagram	photos	captions
map	questions	answers	

Venn Diagram

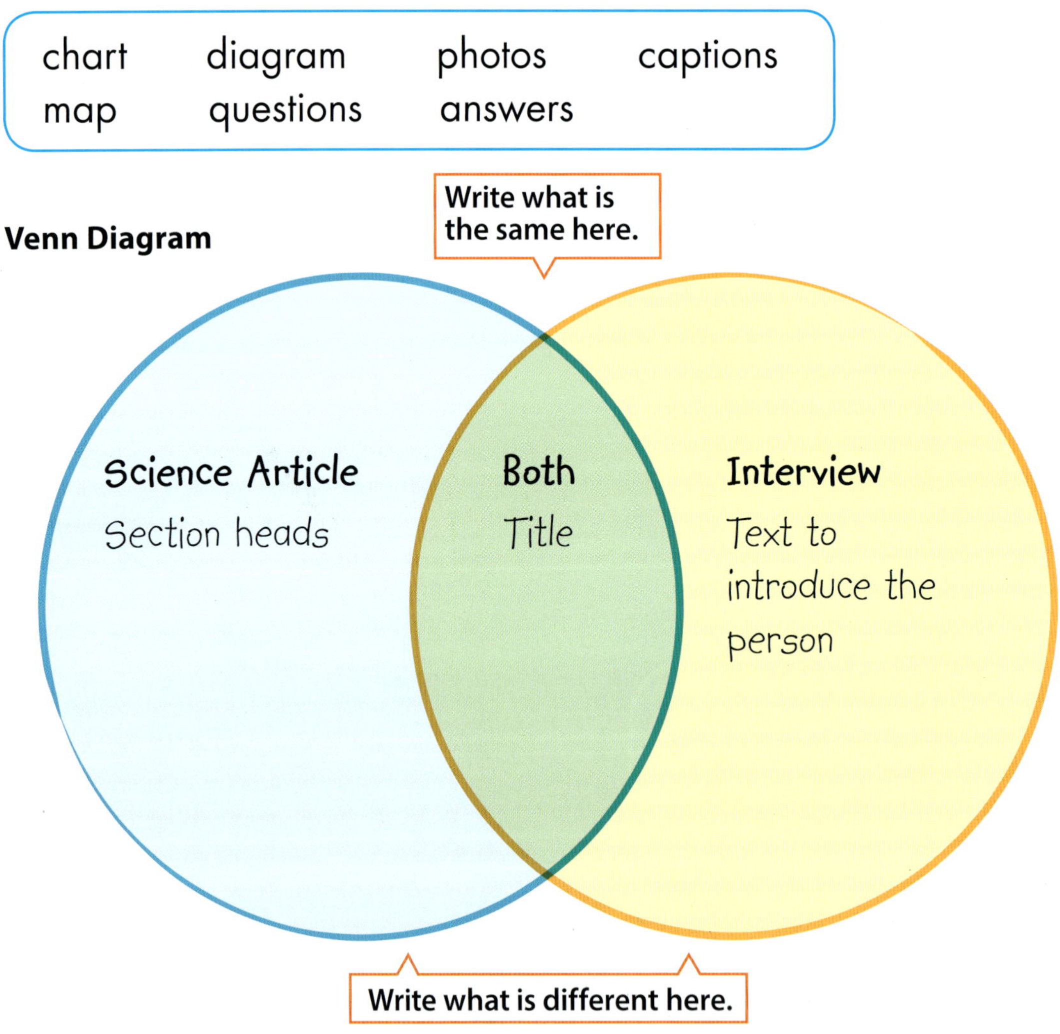

Talk Together

What can cause the **ground** to change? Think about the science article and the interview. Use **Key Words** to explain your ideas.

Possessive Nouns/Adjectives

A **possessive noun** is the name of an owner. A **possessive adjective** can take the place of an owner's name.

apostrophe

Example: **Linda's** family goes to the beach.
Her family goes to the beach.

Grammar Rules Possessive Nouns/Adjectives

	One Owner	More Than One Owner
• Always use an **apostrophe** (') with a possessive noun.	the truck's wheels Corey's shirt	the frogs' log the boys' pebbles
• Be sure to use the correct possessive adjective to tell about the number of owners.	my your his, her, its	our your their

Read Possessive Nouns and Adjectives

Read the sentences. Can you identify one possessive noun and one possessive adjective? Show them to a partner.

Anil's feet sink in the sand. His feet disappear!

Write Possessive Nouns and Adjectives 

Write a caption for each photograph on page 48. Use a possessive noun and a possessive adjective. Read your captions to your partner.

Writing Project

Write as a Reader

Write a Literary Response 

Describe how you felt about one of the selections you read in this unit. Share your opinions with your classmates.

Study a Model

In a literary response, you give your opinions, or personal feelings, about a selection. You support your opinion with details.

Melt the Snow!

by Marisa Montes

reviewed by Rachel Zimmerman

Melt the Snow! is a wonderful play about an ant trapped by a snowflake. I liked it because it was funny and full of surprises.

First, I laughed when Little Ant's leg got caught by the snowflake. I would never have thought that a snowflake could trap an ant!

I was also surprised that none of the strong characters could help Little Ant. For example, Sun couldn't help because it was covered by Cloud. Cloud couldn't move without Wind.

Finally, I liked how the little mouse was the hero. I was happy that he helped Little Ant and saved the day!

The beginning gives a short summary of the play and the writer's opinion.

The writer develops her ideas with details from the play. She presents her ideas in an interesting way.

The ending makes the writing feel complete.

Prewrite

1. **Choose a Topic** With a partner, review the selections in this unit. Talk about how you reacted to each one.

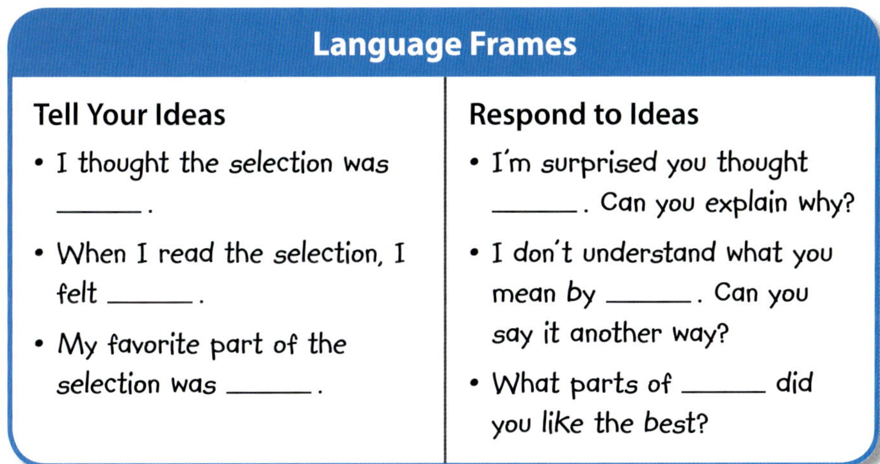

Language Frames	
Tell Your Ideas	**Respond to Ideas**
• I thought the selection was ______.	• I'm surprised you thought ______. Can you explain why?
• When I read the selection, I felt ______.	• I don't understand what you mean by ______. Can you say it another way?
• My favorite part of the selection was ______.	• What parts of ______ did you like the best?

2. **Gather Information** How will you explain your response? Find details in the selection that support your opinion and develop your ideas.

3. **Get Organized** A cause-and-effect chart is one way to organize your thoughts.

Cause-and-Effect Chart

Draft

Use your chart to help you write your draft. State your opinion clearly. Use details from the selection to develop your ideas.

Revise

1. Read, Retell, Respond Read your draft aloud to a partner. Your partner listens and then retells your response. Next, talk about ways to improve your writing.

Language Frames

Retell	Make Suggestions
• You thought the selection was _____. • Your reasons were _____. • Some details you used to support your opinion were _____.	• I'm not sure what your response to _____ was. Can you say it more clearly? • I don't think _____ is a strong reason. • You didn't include many details. Maybe you could add _____.

2. Make Changes Think about your draft and your partner's suggestions. Then use revision marks to make your changes.

- Is your opinion or response clear? If not, try rewording it.

> because it was funny and full of surprises.
> I liked it ~~a lot~~.

- Use details from the selection to support your reasons.

> I was also surprised that none of the strong characters could help Little Ant. For example, Sun couldn't help because it was covered by Cloud.

Edit and Proofread

Work with a partner to edit and proofread your literary response. Check that you used possessive nouns and adjectives correctly. Use revision marks to show your changes.

Punctuation Tip

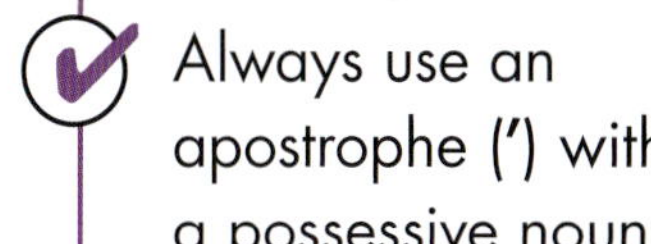

Always use an apostrophe (') with a possessive noun.

- Little Ant's leg
- the students' play

Present

1. **On Your Own** Make a final draft of your literary response. Read it to a partner who wrote about the same selection. Compare your ideas.

Presentation Tips	
If you are the speaker...	**If you are the listener...**
Read slowly and clearly.	Compare the speaker's ideas to your own.
Look up once in a while to make sure your reader understands what you are saying.	Tell whether you agree or disagree, and why.

2. **With a Group** Discuss the selections you read. Ask one another questions about your responses and make comments. You could also start a Reader's Blog and share your ideas that way.

Talk Together

In this unit, you discovered lots of answers to the **Big Question**. Now, use your concept map to discuss the **Big Question** with the class.

Concept Map

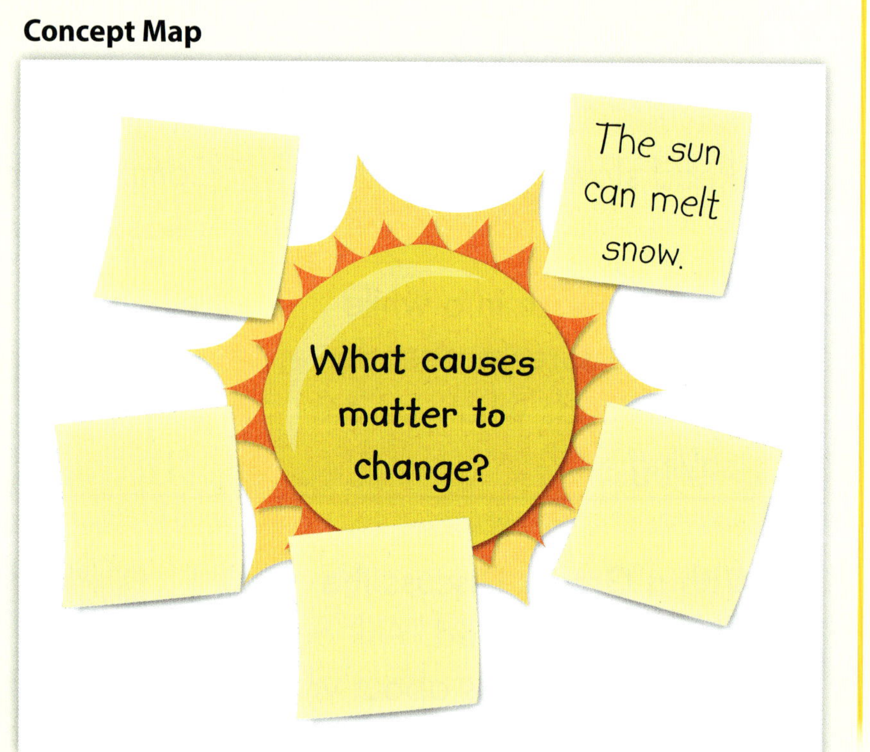

Write an Explanation 

Choose one example from your concept map. Explain how matter changes and what makes it change.

Share Your Ideas

Choose one of these ways to share your ideas about the **Big Question**.

Write It! 

Write a Blog

Think of a time when you went on a camping trip or somewhere else outdoors. Tell how changes in matter affected you. Did it snow? Did the ground become muddy? Share your experience in a blog.

Talk About It!

Give a Weather Broadcast

Work with a partner. Pretend you are a weather team. Report on the hottest or coldest day of the year. Describe what is happening outside.

Do It! 

Perform a Dance

Get together with a group of classmates. Make up a dance to represent a solid, a liquid, or a gas. Perform your dance for the class.

Write It!

Classify Matter

Work with a partner. Look at objects in the classroom or out a window. List some of the objects. Write the name of each object under the word *Liquid*, *Solid*, or *Gas*.

Unit 6

From Past to Present

BIG Question

How can we preserve our traditions?

TRUJILLO, PERU
Children performing a folk dance during a local festival

Unit at a Glance

- **Language Focus**: Ask for and Give Information, Give and Follow Instructions
- **Reading Strategy**: Visualize
- **Phonics Focus**: Prefixes: *un-*, *re-*, *mis-*, *dis-*
- **Topic**: Culture and Traditions

Share What You Know

Do It!

1. **Talk** about traditions in your home.
2. **Share** a song, story, or recipe that you learned from someone in your family.
3. **Draw** a picture that shows something about your traditions and culture.

PART 1 **Language Focus**

Ask for and Give Information

Listen to the dialogue between Jesse and Inez. Then use **Language Frames** with a partner. Ask for and give information about something that you do.

Language Frames

- How do ______?
- It's ______.
- We hear/see/do different ______.

Dialogue 

Social Studies Vocabulary

Key Words
- heritage
- music
- region
- rhythm
- vary

Key Words

Use **Key Words** and other words to talk about **music** in different **regions**.

A mariachi band performs in a plaza in Mexico.

A blues singer in the United States plays a guitar.

A band plays Cuban **rhythms** in Havana.

How does the music **vary**? What music do you like from your **heritage**?

Talk Together

How can you help preserve music you like? Talk with a partner. Use **Key Words** to ask for and give information about the music. Use **Language Frames** from page 76 if you can.

PART 1 Thinking Map

Classify Details

When you **classify details**, you group together details that are alike in some way.

Look at the picture of the band that played at the celebration that Inez went to.

Map and Talk

You can use a web to classify details about something, such as a trip to the fair. Here's how you make one.

The topic of the web goes in the center. The name of each category, or group, goes in a small oval. The details go at the ends of the lines.

Details Web

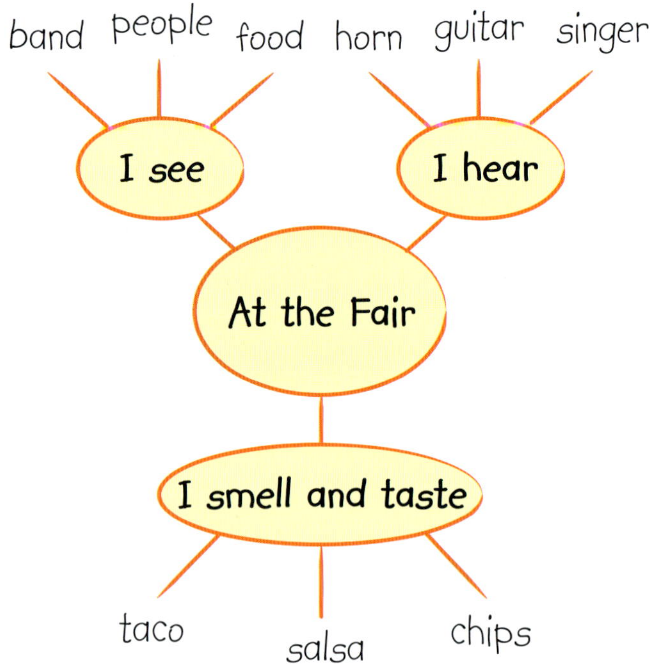

Talk Together

Tell a partner what you see, hear, smell, and taste at a fair or other celebration. Your partner makes a details web.

More Key Words

Use these words to talk about "Shakira, Shakira! A Song" and "Blues Legend: Blind Lemon Jefferson."

express

verb

To **express** a thought or an emotion is to show it. She **expresses** her love for her baby.

feelings

noun

Feelings are how you experience something. Happiness and surprise are kinds of **feelings**.

perform

verb

When you **perform**, you put on a show for a group of people. The girls **perform** on stage.

popular

adjective

When many people like a place or a thing, it is **popular**.

style

noun

Style is a way of doing something. He paints in a colorful **style**.

Talk Together

Make a chart to tell how you feel about each **Key Word**. Compare your chart with a partner's.

Word	Positive (+) Negative (-) Neither (=)	Reason
feelings	=	I think feelings can be both good and bad.

PART 1 **Reading Strategy**

Learn to Visualize

Look at the picture. Find details that show how things look, sound, smell, taste, and feel. Close your eyes and **visualize** the scene. How does this make you feel about the picture?

When you read, you can **visualize** details, too.

How to Visualize

1. Look for details. Find words that tell how things look, sound, smell, taste, and feel.
2. Picture a detail in your mind.
3. Tell how the picture makes you feel. How does it help you make sense of the text?

I read ______.

I picture ______.

I feel ______.

Talk Together

Read Inez's chat. Read the sample visualization. Then use **Language Frames** to visualize details. Tell a partner what you pictured.

Language Frames

- I read ______.
- I picture ______.
- I feel ______.

Online Chat

Inez: I went to the Independence Day fair this weekend.

Alice: Really? Did you have fun?

Inez: Oh, yeah! Bands played. Dancers **performed**. I rode the roller coaster! Woo-whee!

Alice: Did you buy any souvenirs?

Inez: I bought a silver bracelet.

Alice: O-o-o-o! Is it real silver?

Inez: Yes. I had to grab it fast. Lots of people were in the booth pushing and shoving, and the **style** I wanted was really **popular**. I also got a turquoise ring.

Alice: How was the food?

Inez: Awesome! I almost ordered a burger with fries, but I changed my mind. I had a burrito instead. For dessert I had flan, which is a kind of custard.

Alice: Sounds yummy! What was your favorite event?

Inez: The fireworks! Boom! Boom! They were incredible!

Alice: Sounds like a day to remember, Inez.

Inez: It was! I can hardly **express** my **feelings** about Independence Day. It's one of my favorite holidays!

Sample Visualization

"I read the description.

I picture bands playing Mexican music, dancers in bright costumes, and people screaming on a roller coaster ride.

I feel the excitement of the fair."

◄ = A good place to visualize

PART 1 **Phonics Focus**

Prefixes: *un-*, *re-*

untied = not tied

retie = tie again

Listen and Learn

Listen to the picture words for the prefix you hear at the beginning of the words. Choose the prefix *un-* or the prefix *re-* to complete each sentence.

1.

Nan is ___ ___ happy.

2.

We will ___ ___ paint the wall.

3.

I will ___ ___ fill your glass.

4.

The sidewalk has bumps. It is very ___ ___ even.

Talk Together

Listen and read. Find the words with the prefixes *un*- and *re*-.

Over to You

The Magic of Music

How do we remember our heritage? One way is through music. Music can vary from region to region. Different cultures have different styles of music. Music can help us discover our heritage again. To rediscover our traditions is fun. We can revisit our history.

Why do we like music? It's a good way to express feelings. It can also help us change how we feel. If we are unhappy, music can help us feel better. It's almost impossible to stay sad when we hear cheerful music. Music can help us calm down if we feel tense. It's fun to get up and dance to a good rhythm. Dancing is great exercise, too!

Music can bring us together. It can help us learn about the world. It can make us laugh and sing. It can help us recall lost traditions.

Work with a partner.

Find and list the words with the prefixes *un*- and *re*-. Then write these words without the prefixes.

Practice reading words with the prefixes *un*- and *re*- by reading "The Magic of Music" with a partner.

Read Song Lyrics

Genre

Song lyrics are the words of a song. The lyrics of this song express a young girl's thoughts and feelings about a famous singer named Shakira.

Sensory Language

Sensory language helps create pictures in the reader's mind. It tells how things look, sound, smell, taste, and feel.

I listened to your music in my bedroom and *boom, boom, boom!* I was at a Colombian street party.

Yet also, the *twang, twang, twang* of Lebanese string instruments.

Sensory language can describe sounds.

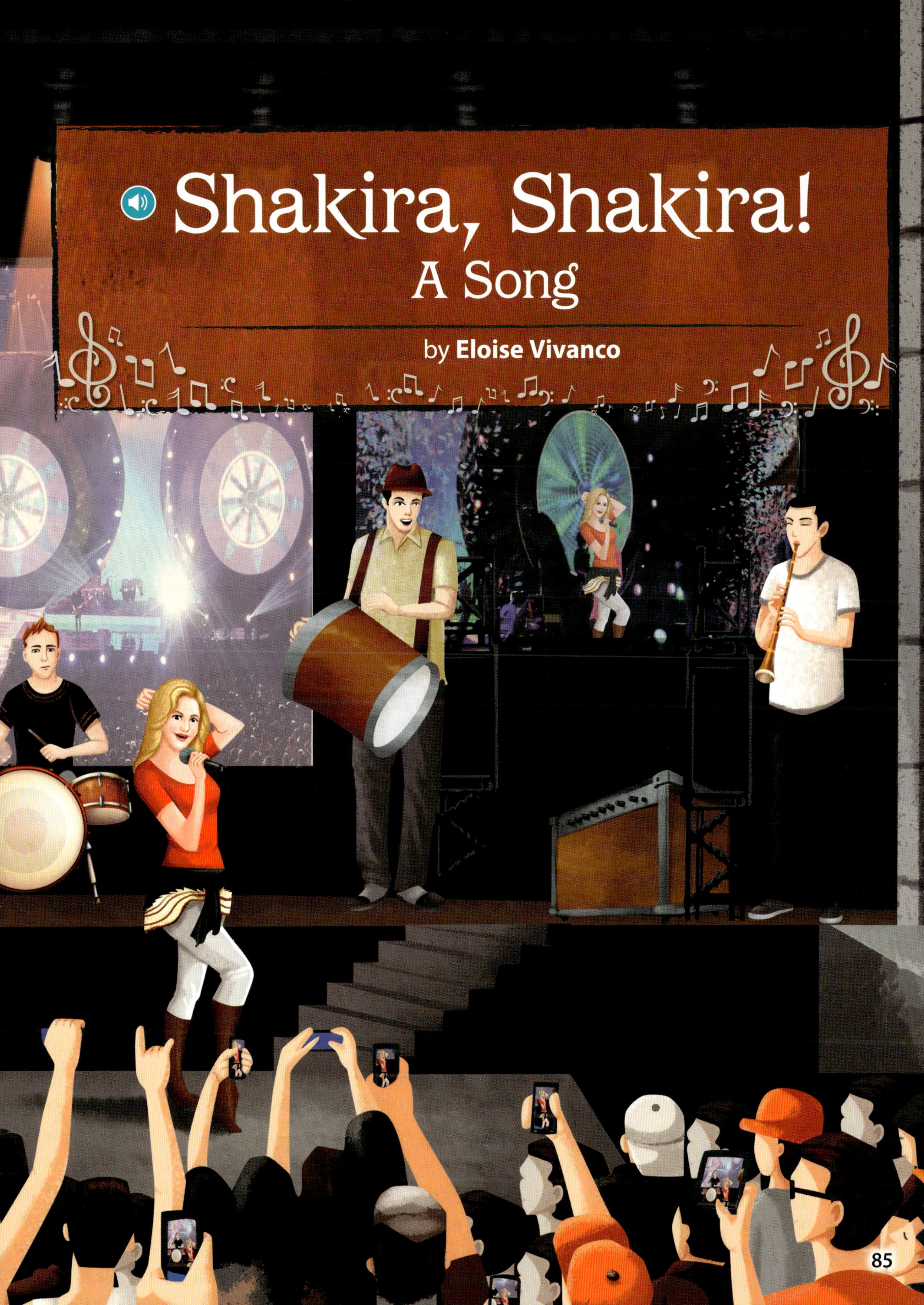
Shakira, Shakira!
A Song
by Eloise Vivanco

Set a Purpose

A girl listens to Shakira's **music**. Read to find out how it affects her.

I listened to the same **music**
day in and day out.

All the bands sounded **like clones**.

Guitars **whining**, electric
keyboards **synthesizing**,

And then I heard you, Shakira.

Shakira was born in Colombia. Her father was born in New York, and her grandparents were from Lebanon. All of these influences can be heard in her music.

day in and day out every day
like clones the same
whining crying, wailing
synthesizing harmonizing

The Latin beats **pulsating** in time with Lebanese drums.

The Spanish lyrics and the Middle Eastern **belly dancing**.

pulsating making rhythmic sounds
belly dancing a traditional Middle Eastern dance

I listened to your **music** in my bedroom
Boom, boom, boom! And I was suddenly at a Colombian street party playing the **tambora**.

Twang, *twang, twang!* I could feel the strings of the **lute**.

The soaring hum of the **mijwiz** as the musician blows softly over the reed.

I was surprised at the way the **rhythm** made my body move, dancing in a way I had never danced before.

Traditional Lebanese musicians and dancers **performing**

tambora Colombian percussion instrument

Twang a strong ringing sound

lute a musical string instrument, similar to a guitar

mijwiz a traditional woodwind musical instrument that has two pipes of equal length

Before You Continue

1. **Classify** Name at least three instruments used in Shakira's **music**.
2. **Visualize** How do you picture the place Shakira is from? What words from the text help you imagine it?

Predict
How will Shakira's **music** make the girl feel?

The **music** of my **homeland** suddenly sounded dull and flat.

Listening to your voice **transported** me to new land.

I dreamed that one day I would visit and feel the magical **rhythms**.

Dance in the street as I imagined the people of Barranquilla did all day!

A Latin party with Lebanese treats!

homeland the place where you were born
transported moved

In your songs, Shakira, I hear
the **fusion** of three **regions**.

So many sounds from each,
coming together
to make **unforgettable** **music**.

Bringing the musical **heritage**
of three different cultures
to the whole world.

And to me, on a **foggy** London day,
so many miles away,

Making me feel happy and bright,
despite the **gloomy** weather.

fusion mixing
unforgettable memorable
foggy misty and wet
gloomy bleak, dreary

Before You Continue

1. **Confirm Prediction** Was your prediction about the girl's **feelings** correct? Explain.
2. **Sensory Language** Reread lines 6–12 on this page. What do you see and hear? How do the words make you feel?

Predict

Shakira's **music** has very strong **rhythms**. What do the girls do when they hear the music?

Swirling, whirling with scarves of silk,
Stereo turned up loud!
Neighbors banging on the door!

Doesn't everyone in Colombia
play the **music** loud?
Any complaints?

The Spanish words, **flowing** and **tumbling**
like a belly dancer's scarf,

Inspiring me to learn your language,
so that I can really know your songs.

Swirling, whirling Spinning, turning
Stereo Machine that plays music
flowing moving smoothly
tumbling rapidly falling or rolling
Inspiring me to Making me want to

Shakira, Shakira, twenty years later and still **performing**, inspiring,
Inspiring my daughters to love **music**.

Different **styles**, sounds that transport them so far away,
As it did for me, so long ago.

Your music **expresses** their **feelings**, and mine.
In time with the **beat**, their hips **sway**, their hearts smile. ❖

beat rhythm

sway a rhythmical side-to-side movement

Before You Continue

1. **Confirm Prediction** What does the woman do when she hears the **rhythms** of Shakira's **music**? Did you predict correctly?
2. **Classify** Shakira's music is a blend of three cultures. What are they?

Meet the Author

Eloise Vivanco

Eloise is from the United Kingdom. She went to college in a very rainy town called Leeds, in the northern part of the country. She first heard Shakira's music with her friend, and they both instantly loved the sound and rhythm. They listened to Shakira all the time in her bedroom and danced with scarves as the girl in the song does. Shakira's music also inspired her to learn Spanish so she could better understand the lyrics.

Shakira ▼

Eloise now lives in Mexico and speaks Spanish fluently, but she still hasn't had the chance to go to a street party in Barranquilla, Colombia. Her eldest daughter likes Shakira's music and wants to see her in concert the next time she comes to Mexico.

Writing Tip

Find places in the song where the writer uses sensory language to show how something sounds or feels. Then write your own sentence. Tell how something in your favorite song sounds or feels.

PART 1 Think and Respond

Key Words	
express	popular
feelings	region
heritage	rhythm
music	style
perform	vary

Talk About It

1. How does the girl feel about Shakira? Find some lines in the **song lyrics** that show the girl's **feelings**.

   The writer _____. Lines that show her feelings are: _____.

2. Pretend that you are a musician playing at one of Shakira's concerts. What might someone ask you about it? **Give information to explain.**

   What instruments _____? How do _____? I play _____. They sound _____.

3. Does the selection have a first-person narrator or a third-person narrator? How do you know?

   It has a _____. I know because _____.

Write About It

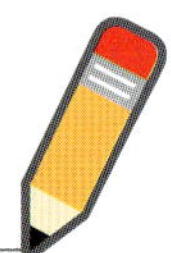

Think of a band or a singer that you like. Write a short persuasive essay to tell why others should listen to this **music**. Write a sentence that **expresses** your opinion. Then write at least three sentences to support your position. Use **Key Words**.

I think everyone _____. First of all, _____.

Reread and Classify

Classify Details

Make a details web for "Shakira, Shakira! A Song." Classify information about Shakira's **music**. Include words that describe the sounds and **feelings** of the music.

Details Web

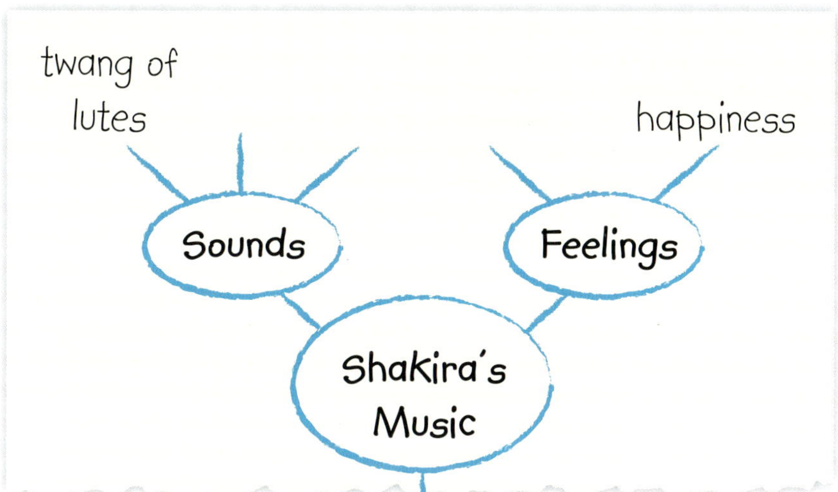

Now use your details web to tell a partner about Shakira's music. Use the sentence frames and **Key Words**. Record your description.

Shakira's music sounds like ______.
Her music inspires feelings of ______.

Fluency

Practice reading with expression. Rate your reading.

Talk Together

How does Shakira preserve the traditions of different countries in her music? Answer the question with a partner. Use **Key Words**.

PART 1 **Word Work**

Playful Language

A **tongue twister** is a phrase or sentence that has many of the same sounds. It's fun to try to say a tongue twister quickly.

Say this tongue twister aloud with a partner.

Sophie says Shakira is a singer with soul and style.

What sounds do you hear that are the same? Say the sentence aloud five times as fast as you can!

Try It Together

Read the tongue twister aloud and complete item 1. Then complete item 2.

The rhythms of rap really rule!

1. **Most of the words begin with the sound of ______ .**
   - **A** l
   - **B** r
   - **C** p
   - **D** th

2. **Which phrase is an example of a tongue twister?**
   - **A** listen to music
   - **B** ten teen tunes
   - **C** rhythm of drums
   - **D** play with the band

Making Connections Read about another musician who added to the musical **heritage** of the United States.

Genre In a **biography**, an author tells about the important events in another person's life.

Blues Legend: Blind Lemon Jefferson

BY LIBBY LEWIS

Blind Lemon Jefferson was a singer and guitar player. He was born on a farm in Texas around 1893. Jefferson **was born blind**, but that didn't stop him from achieving his dreams. He became one of the most **famous** American musicians of all time.

▲ Blind Lemon Jefferson

was born blind could not see
famous well-known

Before You Continue

1. **Make Inferences** What might have made it harder for Jefferson to achieve his dreams? Why?
2. **Classify Details** Find three words on this page that describe Blind Lemon Jefferson.

Music Man

Jefferson started to play guitar and sing when he was a boy. At first, he played **music** on street corners in small towns near his home. Then, as a teenager, he traveled all around the southern states. There, he **performed** his **unique** music for audiences in big cities such as Dallas, Texas.

In 1925, Jefferson went to Chicago, Illinois, to **record** his music. Before his death in 1929, he made more than 100 recordings. This kept his music alive for people to enjoy **decades** later.

Chicago in the 1920s ▶

▲ Southern states

unique special; different
record make copies of
decades many years (one decade = ten years)

The Blues

Blind Lemon Jefferson played a **style** of **music** called "the blues." Blues songs are often about bad luck or trouble, but they can also be fun.

Blues music started from songs sung by enslaved people around the time of the Civil War. The hard work on the farms made them sad and **weary**. They sang the blues to **express** their **feelings**.

Over time, those songs mixed together with church **hymns** and newer types of music.

Many early blues musicians played on street corners. ▶

weary very tired
hymns songs or poems, usually religious

▶ Before You Continue

1. **Classify Details** What kinds of **music** did the blues come from?
2. **Visualize** Who first sang the blues? How does this help you imagine how blues music sounded then?

▼ Record companies used ads to sell Jefferson's **music**.

▼ In the 1920s, artists recorded on record albums like this one.

Keeping the Blues Alive

People all over the country listened to Blind Lemon Jefferson's recordings. He **performed** the blues in a way that no one had ever heard before.

Over time, Jefferson's **style** of blues became very **popular**. He was one of the first African American blues singers to have a big audience. Since then, his **music** has **influenced many musicians**.

influenced many musicians
changed the way people play

▲ B.B. King

▲ Bob Dylan

▲ The White Stripes

Jefferson is gone now, but his blues lives on. He sang with a **high-pitched voice** and played his guitar with **irregular** **rhythm**. Others have tried to follow this **style**, too. Many modern musicians such as Bob Dylan, B.B. King, and The White Stripes have recorded his songs.

People still listen to Jefferson's **music** today. Blind Lemon Jefferson has **truly** helped keep the blues alive. ❖

high-pitched voice voice that was high and sharp, not deep or low

irregular uneven

truly really

Before You Continue

1. **Visualize** Which words help you imagine what Jefferson sounded like when he sang?
2. **Classify Details** Name three musicians or bands who sang Jefferson's songs.

PART 1 Respond and Extend

Key Words	
express	popular
feelings	region
heritage	rhythm
music	style
perform	vary

Compare Language

The song lyrics are literary and the biography is informational, but both texts have similar ideas. Each one tells about a real singer.

With a partner, compare the language in the selections. Complete the T chart. Write three examples of sensory language from the lyrics. Write three facts from the biography.

T Chart

Sensory Language in the Lyrics	Facts in the Biography
1. The Spanish words, flowing and tumbling like a belly dancer's scarf.	1. Jefferson was born in Texas.
2.	2.
3.	3.
4.	4.

Talk Together

How can we preserve our musical traditions? Think about the song lyrics and the biography. Use **Key Words** to talk about your ideas.

Pronoun Agreement

Use the right **subject pronoun** or **object pronoun**.

Grammar Rules Pronoun Agreement

	One	More Than One
• Use for yourself:	I, me	
• Use for yourself and one or more people:		we, us
• Use when you speak to one or more people:	you, you	you, you
• Use for one other person or thing:	he, she, it him, her, it	
• Use for more than one other person or thing:		they, them

Read Pronouns

Read these sentences. Find one subject pronoun and two object pronouns. Show them to a partner.

Shakira started writing songs when she was eight years old, and she still writes songs now. Many people like her. Her music is special to them.

Write Pronouns 

Write two sentences about Shakira or Jefferson. Use a subject and an object pronoun. Check your work with your partner.

Give and Follow Instructions

Language Frames

- First, ______.
- Then, ______.
- Next, ______.
- Finally, ______.

Listen to Ben's song. Then use **Language Frames** to give and follow instructions. Tell a partner how to make something that helps preserve traditions, such as a family album.

Song

SPOON FISH

First, to make a spoon fish,
I find a wooden spoon.
Then, I paint some symbols
Older than the moon.
Next, I add a fish eye bead
And feathers for a fin.
Finally, I hang it up
And watch the spoon
fish spin.

Tune: "The Eensy-Weensy Spider"

Social Studies Vocabulary

Key Words
artist
carve
storyteller
tale
tradition
wood

Key Words

Look at the pictures. Use **Key Words** and other words to talk about **traditions**.

Long ago, **artists** **carved** figures in **wood**.

Some modern artists continue the tradition.

Long ago, people listened to **storytellers**.

People hear some of the same **tales** today.

Talk Together

How do the people in the photos preserve traditions? With a partner, explain what is happening in each photo. Use **Language Frames** and **Key Words**.

PART 2 Thinking Map

Steps in a Process

When you make something, you follow steps in a certain order. One step builds on the other. This is called **steps in a process**.

The pictures show how to make a mask. Look at the four steps.

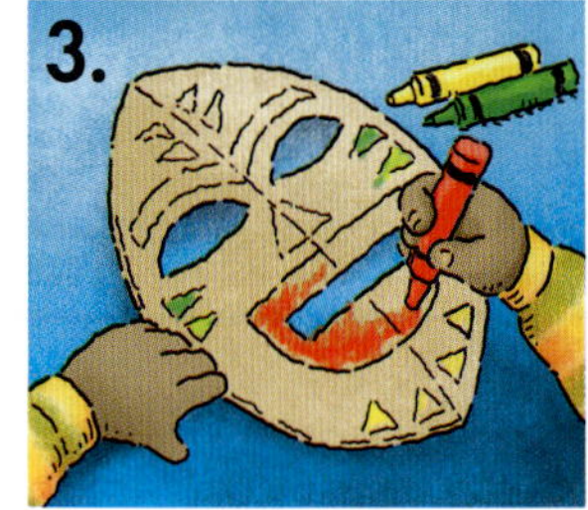

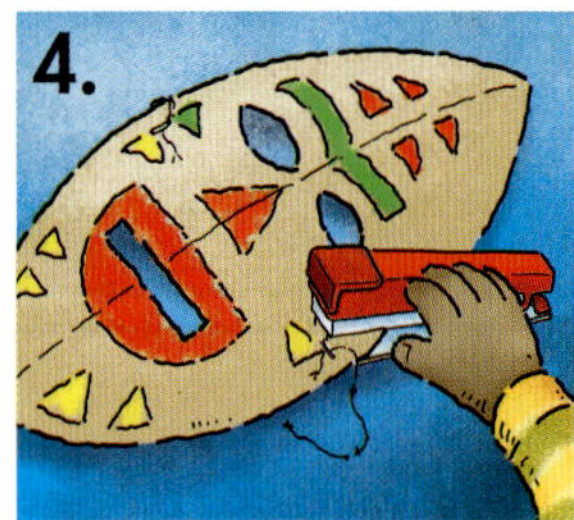

Map and Talk

You can write the steps in a process in a flow chart. Here's how you make one.

Each step goes in a box. The first step goes in the first box. The second step goes in the second box, and so on.

Flow Chart

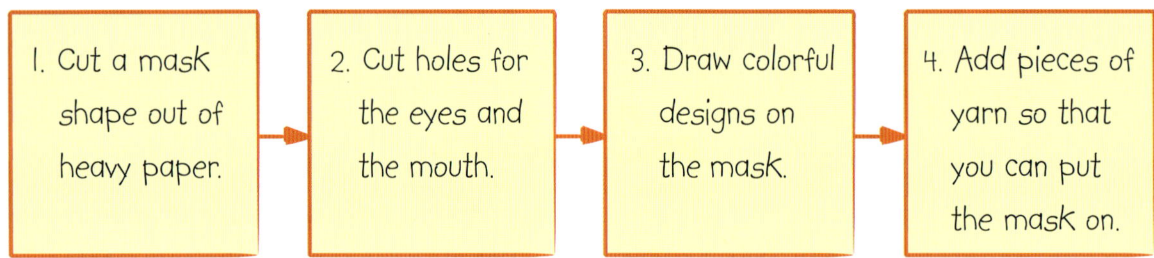

Talk Together

Think of something simple to make. Tell a partner the steps. Your partner restates each step and writes it in a flow chart. Then your partner pantomimes the steps as you read them aloud.

More Key Words

Use these words to talk about "Carving Stories in Cedar" and "Stories to Tell."

communicate

verb

When you **communicate**, you share words or feelings. She **communicates** with a friend.

generation

noun

A **generation** is made up of people born around the same time. They are in different **generations**.

preservation

noun

Preservation is the act of keeping something safe for a long time. The **preservation** of old documents is important.

process

noun

When you follow a **process**, you do something step by step.

represent

verb

To **represent** means to stand for. A heart **represents** love.

Talk Together

Make a Study Card for each **Key Word**. Then compare your cards with a partner's.

Preservation is the act of keeping something safe.

Example: a museum

Not an example: a city dump

PART 2 **Reading Strategy**

Learn to Visualize

Look at the picture and read the caption. Then look away and **visualize** details of the people, place, and event. Make a quick sketch of what you visualized. How does this help you understand the picture?

Ben tells his classmates a traditional tale.

When you read, you can **visualize** to help you understand the text.

How to Visualize

	1. As you read, look for words that describe people, places, and events.	I read ______.
	2. Use the words to create a picture in your mind.	I picture ______.
	3. Draw the picture.	I draw ______.
	4. Ask yourself, "How does this help me understand the text?"	Now I ______.

Language Frames

- I read ______.
- I picture ______.
- I draw ______.
- Now I ______.

Talk Together

Read Ben's instructions. Read the sample visualization. Then use **Language Frames** to visualize as you read. Tell a partner what you pictured.

Instructions

How to Prepare to Tell a Story

1. Find stories you know from your own culture. These are the stories that are passed down from **generation** to generation.
2. Choose the **tale** you want to tell. Stories that have action and humor are the best.
3. Find or draw pictures that **represent** parts of the story. Show the pictures while you tell the story. Pictures help the audience visualize people, places, and events.
4. Practice reading with expression to **communicate** emotion.
5. Practice speaking clearly. If possible, record your story and play it back to hear how your voice sounds.
6. Use body movements to help tell the story. To get the movements right, practice in front of a mirror.

Finally, everyone enjoys listening to stories. So tell stories whenever you can. Use this **process** to prepare. And remember, the **preservation** of traditional tales is serious, but it also can be fun!

Sample Visualization

"I read that stories with action and humor are best.

I picture myself telling a funny story to the class.

I draw my classmates.

Now I understand why it's good to choose stories with humor."

= A good place to visualize

PART 2 **Phonics Focus**

Prefixes: *mis-*, *dis-*

mismatch = match incorrectly

dislike = opposite of like; not like

Listen and Learn

Listen to the words and definitions. Match each word to the correct definition.

1. disagree	spell incorrectly
2. misplace	not obey
3. misuse	not agree
4. disobey	put in the wrong place
5. dishonest	not honest
6. misspell	use badly

Choose two words from the list above. Write your own sentences using the words.

Talk Together

Listen and read. Find the words with the prefixes *mis-* and *dis-*.

Over to You

Cave Paintings

A long time ago, people drew pictures in caves. It is easy to misread these paintings. Some people disagree about what they mean. Are they a way to communicate? Are they the work of storytellers? Are they the work of artists? No one is sure. It is easy to misunderstand their purpose.

How did they even get there? The process wasn't easy. The painters felt discomfort when they drew their paintings. First, they needed to find a cave. Then, they had to get light. There was no light inside caves. Next, they had to get supplies into the cave. Finally, they could create their paintings.

The paintings help us discover things about early people. People may disagree on the meaning of the paintings. But they agree on one thing. They must not disappear.

Work with a partner.

Find the words with the prefixes *mis-* and *dis-*. Make sentences using the words.

Practice reading words with the prefixes *mis-* and *dis-* by reading "Cave Paintings" with a partner.

Read a Descriptive Article

Genre

A **descriptive article** can describe the steps someone uses to do or make something.

Text Features

The **title** tells what the article is about. A **subtitle** gives more information about the title.

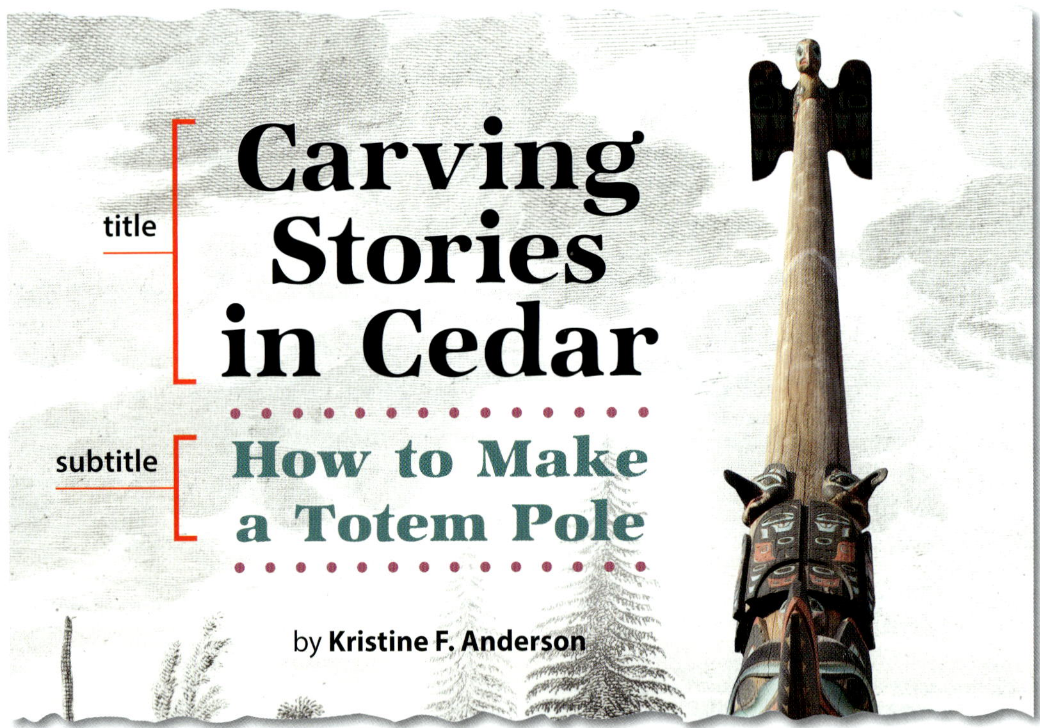

Carving Stories in Cedar

How to Make a Totem Pole

by **Kristine F. Anderson**

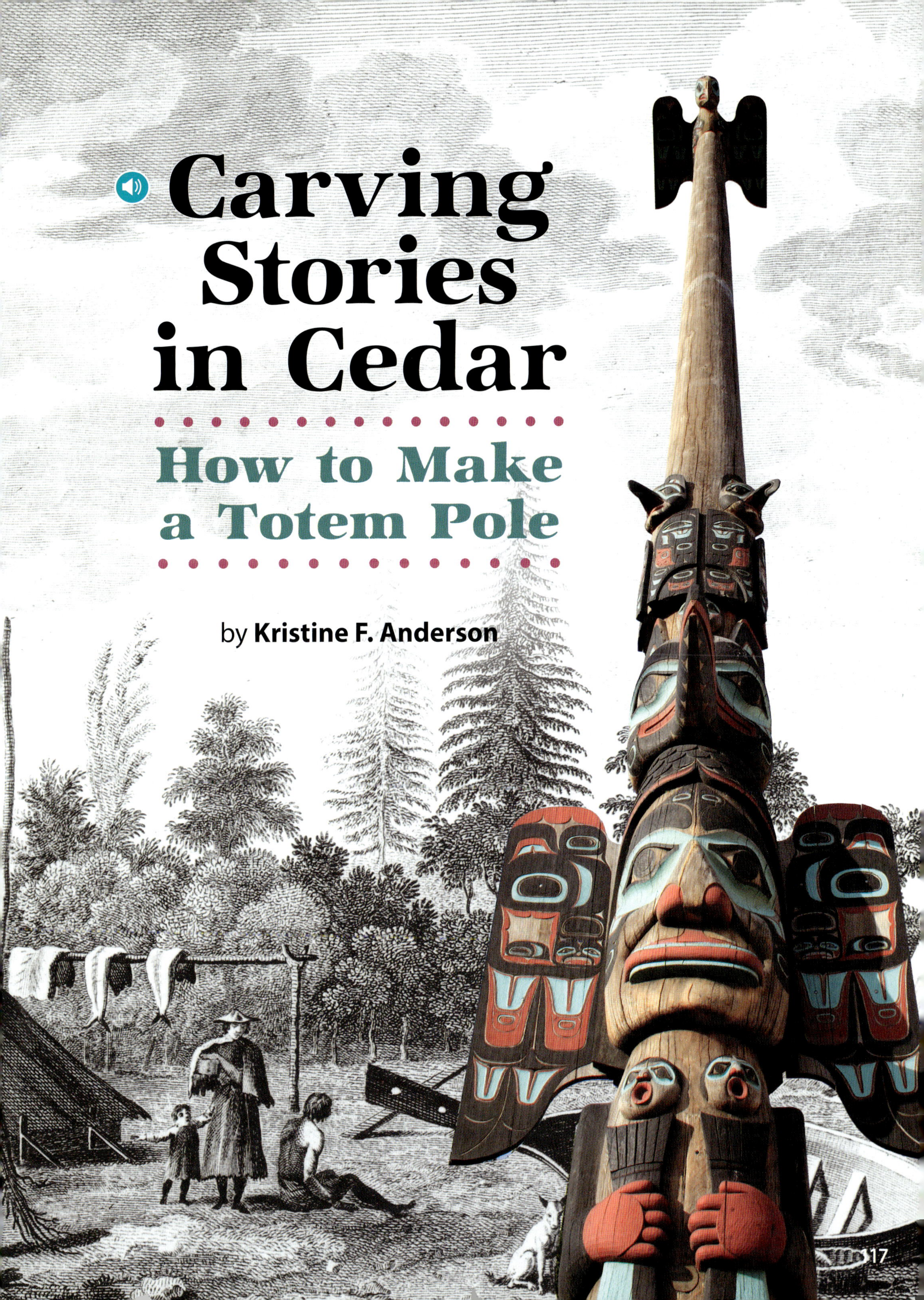

Set a Purpose
Find out what totem poles are and how they are made.

What Is a Totem Pole?

Everyone likes to hear family stories and **legends**. Many **tales** are passed down from **generation** to generation. Hundreds of years ago, **native people** lived along the northwest coast of the United States and Canada. They did not have a written language. These "First People" created a special way to tell their tales and family histories.

legends old tales
native people the first people in the area

Master carvers chose cedar trees from the forests. These trees were tall and straight, and some had red-colored bark. The carvers **carved** pictures into the soft **wood** to **record** family stories. They also carved poles to **honor their chiefs** and other important people who had died. These carvings are called totem poles. They are sometimes called silent books.

This is a finished totem pole. It stands next to uncut cedar trees. ▶

Master carvers People who cut wood really well

record keep and remember

honor their chiefs show that they cared about their leaders

▶ Before You Continue

1. **Visualize** What words help you picture what a cedar tree is like?
2. **Use Text Features** Reread the subtitle of the article. What will you look for as you read on?

How Were the Totem Poles Different?

Each family or **clan** used an animal to **represent** them. The animal stood for something special about **their culture and identity**. So carvers used those animals and other family symbols to create the totem poles. The families placed the tall **sculptures** in front of their homes to show who lived there. They also used the poles like signs to welcome visitors to their villages.

"The poles helped us tell our stories," says Israel Shotridge, a Tlingit carver from Ketchikan, Alaska. "They helped us preserve our culture and identity."

Shotridge in traditional Tlingit clothing ▶

clan group of families living together

their culture and identity who they were and their history

sculptures works of art; carvings

How Do You Carve A Totem Pole?

Shotridge has been **carving** for twenty years. He uses **methods** that were used in the past. "**Tradition** is an important part of what I do," he says.

▲ This is a reproduction of the Sun Raven totem pole. Shortridge finished it in 2003.

Here is how Shotridge makes a totem pole.

1. He chooses a design.

Before he begins carving, Shotridge talks with the person who wants him to carve the pole. They discuss the design. Some of the poles are **reproductions** of old poles. Others are new designs used for businesses, government buildings, and schools.

◀ Two earlier reproductions were made by different **artists** in 1902 and 1938.

methods the same steps
reproductions copies

▸ Before You Continue

1. **Make Inferences** Why is **tradition** important to Shotridge?
2. **Steps in a Process** What do you do first to **carve** a totem pole?

2. He prepares the tree.

Next, Shotridge finds and cuts down a tall, straight cedar tree. He sings special songs that his mother, a **tribal elder**, taught him as he works. Then he **removes the bark**. He draws the design on the **wood** with a special pencil. Sometimes he adds extra pieces of wood to show a bird's wings or a fish's fins.

▲ Shotridge draws a design for a bird's beak.

prepares the tree gets the tree ready
tribal elder wise older person
removes the bark cuts off the outside layer of the tree

3. He carves the pole.

Then Shotridge uses tools, such as an adze and chisel, to carve the design into the wood. An **assistant** may work with him on the larger poles. But even with help, some poles take almost a year to complete.

4. He paints the pole.

Shotridge paints his poles in the traditional colors of red, teal, blue, and black. Early carvers made their paints from **local minerals**, such as copper and iron, mixed with salmon eggs. But Shotridge, like most modern carvers, buys his paint.

▲ Sue Shotridge paints in traditional colors.

assistant helper
local minerals materials from nature

Before You Continue

1. **Details** What tools does Shotridge need to make a totem pole?
2. **Steps in a Process** What must Shotridge do before he starts carving?

5. People raise the totem pole.

When the pole is almost finished, plans are made to raise it. **Cranes** lift big poles into place. The poles often weigh more than a thousand pounds! Smaller poles are raised by hand.

"We usually raise poles the **old-fashioned** way," says Shotridge. "We use **lots of manpower** and ropes."

▲ **People use ropes to raise a totem pole.**

Cranes Large machines used to lift heavy objects

old-fashioned old

lots of manpower the strength of many people

▲ These traditional costumes are worn to a potlatch.

6. Everyone celebrates!

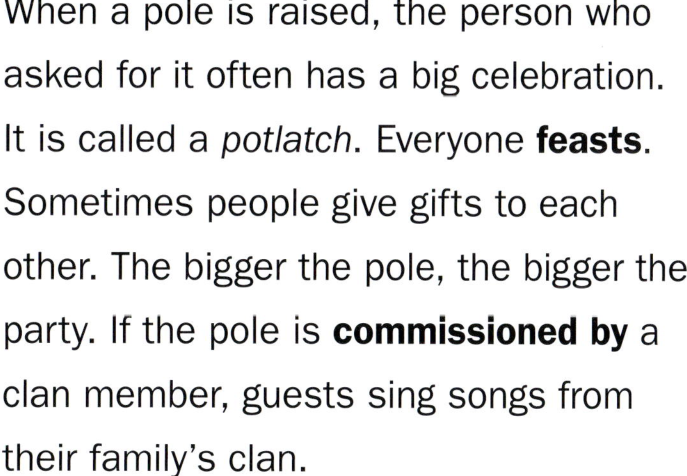

When a pole is raised, the person who asked for it often has a big celebration. It is called a *potlatch*. Everyone **feasts**. Sometimes people give gifts to each other. The bigger the pole, the bigger the party. If the pole is **commissioned by** a clan member, guests sing songs from their family's clan.

Once the pole has been raised, another silent book stands to tell the story of the people of the Northwest.

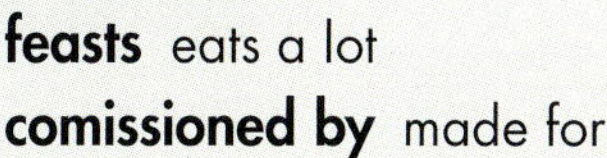

feasts eats a lot
comissioned by made for

Before You Continue

1. **Visualize** Picture yourself at a potlatch. What do you see, hear, smell, taste, and feel?
2. **Cause/Effect** What are two ways the size of the pole can affect what happens in the last two steps?

Set a Purpose

Now read a legend that reminds people to value the gifts of others.

Shotridge's totem pole shows Fog Woman's gift of salmon.

The Legend of Raven and Fog Woman

retold by **Susan Blackaby**

illustrated by **Amanda Hall**

One day long ago, Raven went fishing. He needed to get ready for winter. Again and again he **cast** his nets, but he didn't catch a single fish. As he **paddled** toward shore, Raven became lost in **a swirl of fog**. The fog was so thick that Raven didn't notice the beautiful woman sitting next to him. Then suddenly she spoke.

"**Lend** me your hat," she said.

cast threw

paddled rowed

a swirl of fog clouds close to the ground that are hard to see through

Lend Give

Raven took off his hat, and Fog Woman used it to gather up the fog. When the sky cleared, Raven returned home with the **mysterious** woman. Soon after, Raven and Fog Woman were married.

Winter arrived, and food was **scarce**. One rainy morning, Raven felt grumpy and hungry. He **scolded** Fog Woman, who was making a basket.

"You're wasting your time," snapped Raven. "What good is an empty basket?"

Fog Woman didn't answer.

mysterious unusual, interesting
scarce hard to find
scolded spoke angrily to

Fog Woman filled the new basket with water and washed her hands in it. When she dumped the water back into the creek, four silvery **salmon** slipped out.

Raven asked, "How did you do that?"

Fog Woman didn't answer.

Day after day she filled the basket with water, and soon the creek **ran bright with** salmon. No one in the village went hungry.

But Raven wasn't **satisfied**. He clawed the ground with his feet and flapped his wings angrily.

salmon fish
ran bright with was full of
satisfied happy; pleased

"Tell me your secret," Raven **demanded**.

Fog Woman wouldn't answer.

Raven **lost his temper**. "If you won't tell me, then go!" he shouted.

As Fog Woman left, the salmon rushed after her. Raven rushed after her, too. He reached for her, but he couldn't hold on. Fog Woman had turned into **mist**.

Raven lost Fog Woman forever, but each year she sends a basket of salmon so that no one in the village goes hungry. ❖

demanded ordered
lost his temper became angry
mist small drops of water

Before You Continue

1. **Clarify** Why did Fog Woman leave Raven?
2. **Visualize** What do you think the villagers did when they discovered all the salmon? Draw the scene.

PART 2 **Think and Respond**

Talk About It

Key Words	
artist	represent
carve	storyteller
communicate	tale
generation	tradition
preservation	wood
process	

1. As you read the **descriptive article**, what did you visualize? Give an example.

   I pictured ____.

2. With a partner, pretend to make a totem pole. **Give and follow instructions**. Use the article to help you.

   First, ____. Then, ____. Next, ____. Finally, ____.

3. Look back at the picture of the totem pole on page 126. How does it **represent** the story of Raven and Fog Woman?

   The totem pole has ____. It shows ____.

Write About It

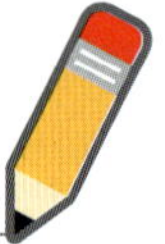

It takes a lot of time and work to make a totem pole. What would you like to ask the **artist** about the **process**? Write one question for each step. Use **Key Words**.

1. What ____?
2. How ____?

Reread and Explain

Steps in a Process

"Carving Stories in Cedar" tells how people make and display a totem pole. Write the steps in a flow chart. To help you remember, look at the numbers next to the headings on pages 121–125.

Flow Chart

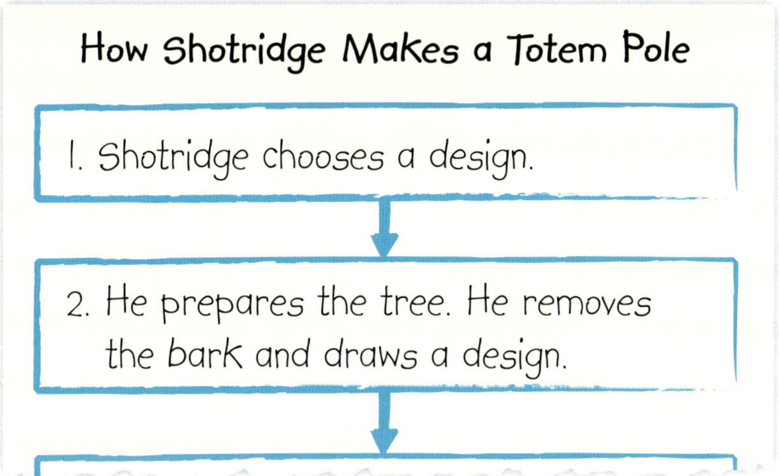

Use your flow chart to explain the steps to a partner. Your partner restates each step and pantomimes it. Use the sentence frames and **Key Words**. Record your explanation.

Fluency

Practice reading with intonation. Rate your reading.

Talk Together

How do **artists** and **storytellers** preserve **traditions**? Use **Key Words** to help you write your ideas. Share your ideas with the class.

PART 2 **Word Work**

Homophones

Homophones are words that sound the same, but have different spellings and meanings.

This **tale** is about a clever fox.

Meaning: a story

The fox has a long, fluffy **tail**.

Meaning: an animal's body part

Try It Together

Read the sentences. Then answer the questions.

I think it would be fun to carve a whale out of wood. My friend carved one and won a prize.

1. **What word is a homophone for would?**
   - **A** prize
   - **B** carve
   - **C** wood
   - **D** whale

2. **What word is a homophone for one?**
   - **A** fun
   - **B** out
   - **C** won
   - **D** would

NATIONAL GEOGRAPHIC EXCLUSIVE

Making Connections Read about another way to share **traditions**.

Genre A **profile** is nonfiction. It gives facts about a person and his or her life. A **folk tale** is an old story that tells why something is the way it is.

Stories to Tell

by **Janine Boylan**

When Elizabeth Lindsey was seven years old, the **elders** predicted that she would **keep the voices of her ancestors alive**. When her father asked her what she would do in her life, Elizabeth said she would tell stories.

Elizabeth Lindsey was born and raised in Hawaii. ▶

elders older people

keep the voices of her ancestors alive share her family's history and traditions with others

Before You Continue

1. **Use Text Features** Read the title. How does Elizabeth keep her ancestors' voices alive?
2. **Make Inferences** How do you think the elders felt about what Elizabeth wanted to do?

The moon over Kalalau Beach in Kauai, Hawaii.

Like other **native Hawaiian** children, Elizabeth was raised by a group of elders as well as her parents. The elders teach the children how the **cycles of the moon** can show them the best times to plant and fish. They teach the children to respect nature, too. The children learn to take only what they need and return the rest.

native Hawaiian born and raised in Hawaii

cycles of the moon changes in the way the moon looks at night

Elizabeth listens to a legend told by an elder.

During sharing time in the fourth grade, Elizabeth loved to tell stories about the people she cared about. As she grew, she realized she wanted to **preserve** the stories from native people around the world, like those who had raised her.

Now, Elizabeth travels to listen to stories from native **cultures** few people know about. She says, "The more I learn about other people, the more amazed I am at how much we are alike."

"The Rainbow Bridge" on the following pages is just one of the many stories Elizabeth tells to share her Hawaiian culture.

preserve save

cultures groups of people with the same history and way of life

Before You Continue

1. **Visualize** If you traveled with Elizabeth, what do think you would see and do? Sketch your ideas. Then describe your picture.
2. **Draw Conclusions** Do you think Elizabeth likes her job as a **storyteller**? Explain.

▸ **Set a Purpose**
Read this folk **tale** to find out how a rainbow came to be.

THE RAINBOW BRIDGE

A NATIVE FOLK TALE FROM HAWAII • ILLUSTRATED BY BELLE YANG

A long time ago in Hawaii, the people **set out** in their **canoes**. They rowed a long way north of their home. They rowed for days and days. The air got colder. The days **grew shorter**. Finally, they reached a new, cold place.

Wonderful people came to greet them. These people took them into their homes. They fixed their **worn** canoes. They treated the Hawaiians like family.

set out left their homes
canoes long, thin boats
grew shorter had less and less sunshine
worn broken

At first, the Hawaiians loved this new place. They were happy. They married. They had children.

But then they remembered the warm, tropical land where they had come from. The more they remembered this land, the more they wanted to return there with their new families.

But they loved their new home, too. They knew that if they rowed back to Hawaii, they might never be able to return to this land.

They hoped **silently** for a way to return to their old home. They also wanted a way to travel back to their new home.

silently without telling anyone

▶ Before You Continue

1. **Use Text Features** Read the title of the folk tale. What do you think a rainbow bridge is?
2. **Compare and Contrast** How was the Hawaiian people's new home different from their old home? How was it the same?

Predict
Do you think the people will find a way to travel back to their old home?

Kind-hearted Weasel heard their wishes. He had an idea.

Weasel began to play his flute. As the notes filled the air, a **colorful arc** rose from the land and into the sky. Weasel played until the bridge grew high above the ocean. It ended beyond where they could see. Weasel explained that this bridge would take them between their new and old homes.

The people were so excited they ran toward the bridge. They grabbed their children's hands. They grabbed their wives' and husbands' hands. "When you climb this bridge, do not look down," Weasel warned them. But they did not listen.

Kind-hearted Caring, sympathetic
colorful arc rainbow

Some people got to the top of the bridge. They looked down. The ocean was far below them. They **got dizzy** and fell into the water. These people became dolphins who could travel the seas.

The people used the rainbow bridge to travel between their two homes. The dolphins swam from place to place.

Now people know that the rainbow **represents the colors of people** around the world. It also represents the bridge that brings them together.

Where I love there are rainbows.
Where I live is a place of ***harmony***
that follows whatever is.

—traditional Hawaiian saying ❖

got dizzy felt strange

represents the colors of people stands for all the different kinds of people

harmony peace

Before You Continue

1. **Confirm Prediction** Did the Hawaiian people find a way to travel back to their old home? Explain.
2. **Visualize** What do you think it would it be like to walk across a rainbow bridge? Describe what you would see and feel.

PART 2 **Respond and Extend**

Compare Themes

Key Words

artist	represent
carve	storyteller
communicate	tale
generation	tradition
preservation	wood
process	

What is the theme, or main message, of "The Legend of Raven and Fog Woman"? What is the theme of "The Rainbow Bridge"?

Make a theme web for each story. In your own words, write the theme and details that support the theme.

Theme Web

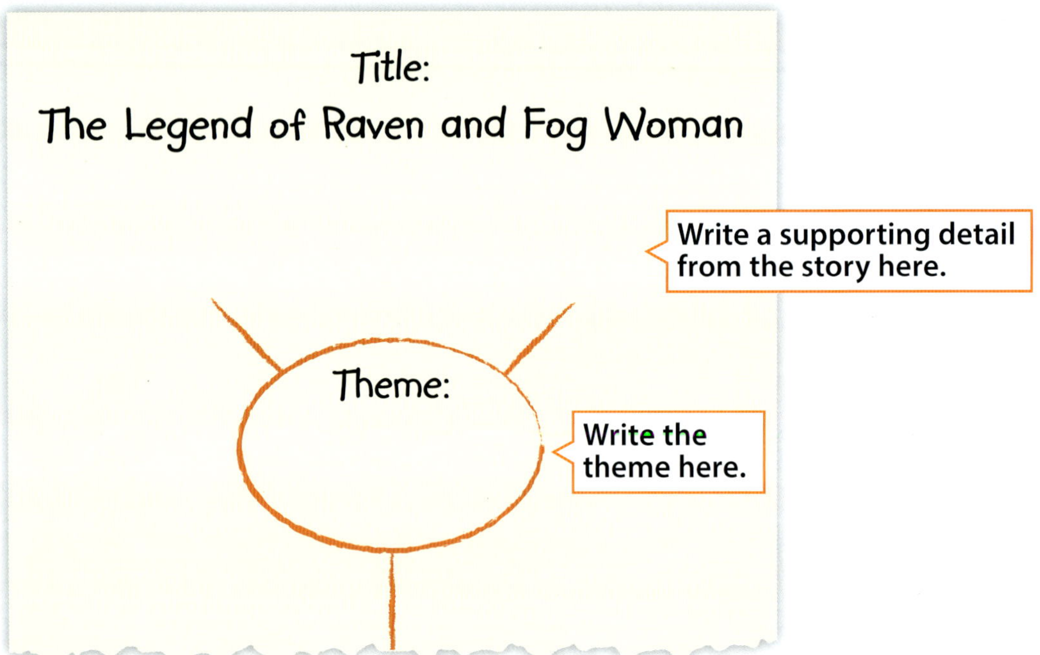

Talk Together

Share your theme webs with a partner. Discuss how the themes of the two **tales** are alike and different. Use **Key Words** to talk about your ideas.

Pronoun Agreement

Possessive pronouns tell who or what owns something. Be sure to use the right possessive pronoun.

Grammar Rules **Pronoun Agreement**

• For yourself, use **mine**.	The pencil is **mine**.
• For yourself and one or more people, use **ours**.	The tools are **ours**.
• When you speak to one or more people, use **yours**.	Is that design **yours**?
• For one other person or thing, use **his**, **hers**, or **its**.	The hat is **his**. She likes **hers**.
• For two or more other people or things, use **theirs**.	The costumes are **theirs**.

Read Possessive Pronouns

Read these sentences. Find two possessive pronouns.

We made paper totem poles like theirs. This one is mine.

Write Possessive Pronouns

With a partner, talk about the photograph on the top of page 125. Then write a sentence for the photo. Use a possessive pronoun.

Writing Project

Write Like a Reporter

Write an Interview

Interview someone who helps preserve a special tradition. Share your interviews with classmates and others in your school.

Study a Model

In an interview, you ask a person questions to get information. Read Kia's interview with her aunt, who makes Hmong story cloths.

The first paragraph tells who is interviewed and what the interview is about.

Each **answer** gives the person's exact words.

The **questions** are organized in a natural order. One question flows into the next one.

Aunt Yi's Story Cloths

by Kia Lau

The Hmong people of Laos are known for their beautiful story cloths. My Aunt Yi makes these cloths. I asked her about them.

Kia: What are story cloths?
Aunt Yi: They are a special type of needlework. The pictures that I sew into the cloths tell stories about our people.

Kia: When did you start making them?
Aunt Yi: Oh, it was years ago, when I was a young girl living in a Thai refugee camp.

Kia: Why do you still make them?
Aunt Yi: People around the world now admire Hmong story cloths. I am proud to be one of the artists who helps preserve this tradition.

Prewrite

1. **Choose a Topic** What traditions would you like to learn about? Who could you interview? Discuss your ideas with a partner.

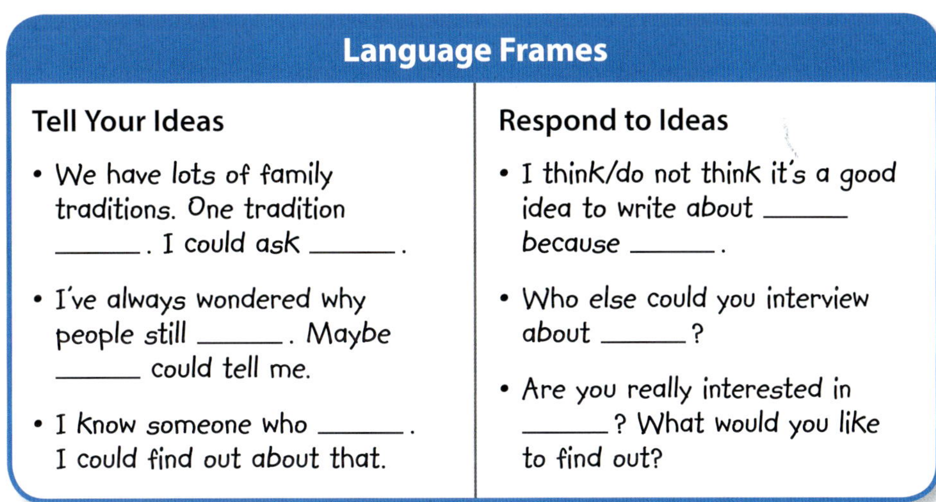

Language Frames

Tell Your Ideas	Respond to Ideas
• We have lots of family traditions. One tradition ______. I could ask ______.	• I think/do not think it's a good idea to write about ______ because ______.
• I've always wondered why people still ______. Maybe ______ could tell me.	• Who else could you interview about ______?
• I know someone who ______. I could find out about that.	• Are you really interested in ______? What would you like to find out?

2. **Gather Ideas** Now think about your first paragraph and questions you want to ask.

3. **Get Organized** Use a details web to organize your ideas.

Details Web

Draft

Use your details web to help you plan your opening paragraph and questions. After the interview, prepare a draft. Remember to write the person's own words for the answers.

Writing Project, continued

Revise

1. **Read, Retell, Respond** Read your draft aloud to a partner. Your partner listens and then retells what the interview is about. Next, talk about ways to improve your writing.

Language Frames

Retell	Make Suggestions
• You interviewed _____. • The tradition you asked about was _____. • The questions _____.	• The questions didn't seem to be in a natural order. Could you organize them differently? • I didn't understand _____. Did you write down the answer correctly?

2. **Make Changes** Think about your draft and your partner's suggestions. Then use revision marks to make your changes.

   • Are your questions in a natural order that flows? If not, try changing the order.

> **Kia: When did you start making them?**
>
> **Aunt Yi:** Oh, it was years ago in a Thai refugee camp.
>
> **Kia: What are story cloths?**
>
> **Aunt Yi:** They are a special type of needlework.

   • Did you write the person's exact words? Check your notes and make corrections.

> ^, when I was a young girl living
>
> **Aunt Yi:** Oh, it was years ago ^ in a Thai refugee camp.

Edit and Proofread

Work with a partner to edit and proofread your interview. Pay special attention to pronouns. Use revision marks to show your changes.

Grammar Tip

Make sure you use the right pronoun. Look back at pages 107 and 141 if you need help.

Present

1. **On Your Own** Make a final copy of your interview. Then choose a way to share it with your classmates. You may want to read the interview aloud with a partner and record it.

Presentation Tips	
If you are the speaker...	**If you are the listener...**
Pause after you finish reading a question or the answer to a question.	Think about whether the interviewer asked good questions. What might you have asked instead?
Change your pitch and tone to match reading a question or reading an answer.	What else would you like to know about this tradition? Ask the speaker for more details.

2. **With a Group** Collect all the interviews in a book called "Let's Preserve Traditions." Display the book in a classroom reading station or in your school library along with any recordings.

Talk Together

In this unit, you found lots of answers to the **Big Question**. Now, use your concept map to discuss the **Big Question** with the class.

Concept Map

Write a Personal Narrative 

Use your concept map to help you think of a time when you preserved a tradition. Write a personal narrative about it.

Share Your Ideas

Choose one of these ways to share your ideas about the **Big Question**.

Write It!

Write Song Lyrics

Think about one of your favorite singers or musicians. What is this person's style of music? Write song lyrics about the person. Share your lyrics with the class.

Talk About It!

Interview a Musician

Work in a group of four. Two group members pretend to be Shakira and Jefferson. The other two interview them. One question could be, "Why would you like to pass your music on to future generations?"

Do It!

Make Instructions

Think of something traditional that a family member taught you to do. Write or draw a short set of steps. Read the instructions to a partner. Your partner restates each step and pantomimes it. Switch roles.

Write It!

Write a Letter

Pretend you are making a time capsule. Think of a tradition that you want to save. Write a letter to future children. Tell why it is important to preserve this tradition.

Dear Kids of the Future,

We need to preserve blues music. It tells stories of how people have survived.

Unit 7

Blast! Crash! Splash!

BIG Question

What forces can change Earth?

REUNION ISLAND, FRANCE
A scientist moving towards a volcano to examine lava

Unit at a Glance

- **Language Focus**: Tell an Original Story, Express Opinions and Ideas
- **Reading Strategy**: Draw Conclusions, Form Generalizations
- **Phonics Focus**: Suffixes: *-sion, -tion, -ous*; Syllable Pattern: Consonant + *-le, -al, -el*
- **Topic**: Forces of Nature

Share What You Know

Do It!

1. **Think** of a force of nature, such as an earthquake or a storm, that you have read about or seen on TV.
2. **Draw** a picture of it.
3. **Share** your picture with the class. Explain your drawing.

PART 1 **Language Focus**

Tell an Original Story

Listen to Jenny's poem. Then use **Language Frames** to tell a story of your own.

Language Frames

- This story is about ______.
- It happens ______.
- First, ______.
- Then, ______.

A Scary Ride

This story is about a boy
With truly unruly hair.
It happens in a hot volcano.
You wouldn't think he'd dare!

First, he rides his tiny red cart
Down tunnels long and deep.
Soon, bubbling magma, thick as mud,
Begins to warm his feet.

Then, suddenly the place erupts!
Upward shoots his cart.
Bump! He lands—back on track,
In an amusement park.

Science Vocabulary

Key Words

Key Words	
erupt	magma
flow	ocean
island	rock
lava	volcano

Look at this diagram. Use **Key Words** and other words to talk about what happens when a **volcano** **erupts**.

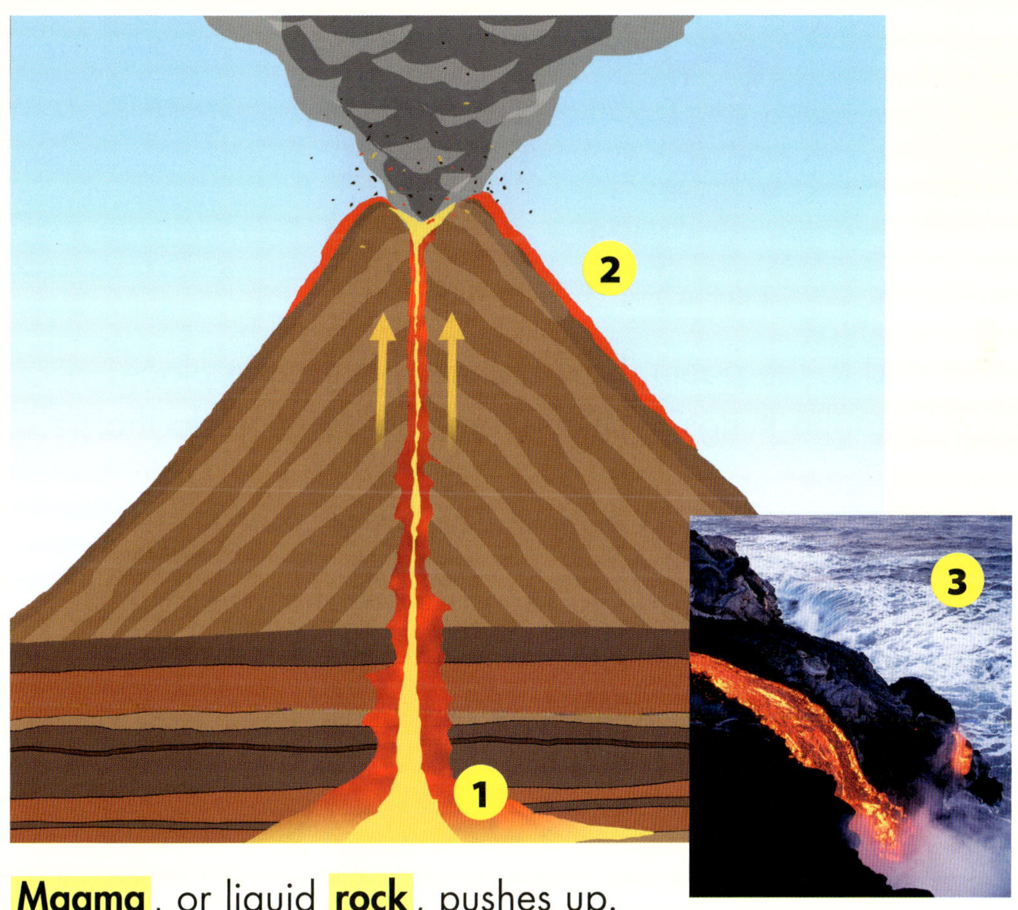

1. **Magma**, or liquid **rock**, pushes up.
2. **Lava** **flows** out.
3. Lava cools in the **ocean**. Over time, this can form **islands**.

Talk Together

With a partner, tell an original story about forces that change something on Earth. Who is the story about? Where does it happen? Use **Language Frames** from page 150 and **Key Words**.

PART 1 **Thinking Map**

Imagery

Words can create pictures in people's minds. Word pictures, or **imagery**, tell how things look, sound, smell, taste, and feel.

Look at these pictures from Jenny's poem. Read the labels.

As you listened to the poem, how did you picture the place, the person, and the things? Which words helped you do that?

Map and Talk

You can use an imagery chart to record word pictures from a story. To make one, write categories at the top of the chart. Then find word pictures for each category.

Imagery Chart

Place	Person	Thing
hot volcano	boy with truly unruly hair	tiny red cart
tunnels long and deep	magma warms his feet	bubbling magma, thick as mud

Talk Together

Make up a story with a partner. Use word pictures to describe places, people, and things. Record the word pictures in an imagery chart.

More Key Words

Use these words to talk about "An Island Grows" and "Volcano Views."

core
noun

The **core** is the middle of something. An apple **core** is the center part of an apple.

create
verb

To **create** means to make something new. She **creates** a picture.

develop
verb

When something **develops**, it grows over time. The small plant will **develop** into a large tree.

force
noun

Force means power or strength. The **force** of the wind bends this tree.

pressure
noun

When one thing pushes against another, it makes **pressure**. **Pressure** from the nutcracker causes the nuts to crack open.

Talk Together

Write a sentence for each **Key Word**. Include clues. Copy each sentence with a blank for the **Key Word**. A partner fills in the missing word.

The center of Earth is the ____.

PART 1 Reading Strategy

Learn to Draw Conclusions

Look at the picture. The land looks bad, but new plants are growing. Think about how those parts of the picture go with one another. Then **draw a conclusion**, or decide something about what the picture shows.

When you read, you **draw conclusions**, too.

How to Draw Conclusions

	1. Notice an important idea in the text.	I read ______.
	2. Look for another idea that you think is important.	I also read ______.
	3. How do the ideas go with one another? Put the ideas together to make a conclusion about the text.	I connect the ideas and conclude ______.

Talk Together

Read Jenny's description of a volcanic explosion. Read the sample conclusion. Then use **Language Frames** to draw conclusions as you read. Tell a partner about them.

Language Frames

- I read ______.
- I also read ______.
- I connect the ideas and conclude ______.

Description

Mount St. Helens

Mount St. Helens is a **volcano** in Washington State in the USA. It used to be a pretty place. It had green forests, clear rivers, and lakes. Lots of wildlife lived in the region.

Sample Conclusion

"I read that Mount St. Helens is a volcano.

I also read that it used to be a pretty place.

I connect the ideas and conclude that Mount St. Helens erupted and ruined the area."

The volcano had **erupted** in 1800, followed by many small eruptions. By 1857 it was quiet again. Then on March 15, 1980, earthquakes began to shake the mountain. Ash and steam came up through the volcano's **core** with great **force**. Gas eruptions **created** two more craters near the top.

Around this time, a huge bulge **developed** on the side of the mountain. It grew larger and larger, like a lopsided balloon. ◄

Finally, on May 18, the **pressure** became too strong. BLAM! WHAM! Two mighty eruptions blew the top off the mountain.

Steam and ash rose thousands of feet into the sky. Hot mudflows raced down the mountainsides. Mud and **rocks** flattened the forests. They blocked the rivers. They smothered most of the wildlife. Mount St. Helens wasn't a pretty place anymore. ◄

◄ = A good place to draw a conclusion

PART 1 **Phonics Focus**

Suffixes: -sion, -tion, -ous

collision

eruption

joyous

Listen and Learn

Listen to each word. Then sort the words according to their suffixes.

attention	explosion	vacation	famous
division	nervous	dangerous	direction

-sion	**-tion**	**-ous**
______	______	______
______	______	______
______	______	______

Choose one word from each column above. Write your own sentence for each word.

Talk Together

Listen and read. Find the words that end with the suffixes *-sion*, *-tion*, and *-ous*.

Over to You

The Story of Pompeii

This story is about the city of Pompeii. Pompeii disappeared. It happened on AD August 24, 79. That was the day Mt. Vesuvius erupted. It was a serious eruption.

First, there was a loud explosion. Then, smoke and dangerous gas filled the air. Lava flowed down the volcano. More than a million tons of ash shot into the air. The ash blew in the direction of Pompeii. It fell like black snow. The people ran from it. The sky became as dark as night. Some people escaped. Most did not. Ash covered the city. The day after the eruption, the city was gone. It was completely buried in ash.

The ash kept the city as it was. People found the buried city in 1748. They found houses. They found streets. They found tables and chairs. They found dishes and cups on tables. They found bread in ovens. They couldn't believe what they found. Today, many people visit to see the buried city of Pompeii.

Work with a partner.

Find and list the words with the suffixes *-sion*, *-tion*, and *-ous*. Challenge each other to make new sentences using the words.

Practice reading words with the suffixes *-sion*, *-tion*, and *-ous* by reading "The Story of Pompeii" with a partner.

Read a Narrative Poem

Genre

A **narrative poem** is a poem that tells a story.

Elements of Poetry

Rhythm is the beat of the words in a poem. **Rhyme** is the repetition of sounds at the ends of words.

The lines have a quick, sharp rhythm, or beat.

Deep, deep beneath the sea...
Stone breaks.
Water quakes.

Rhyming words have the same ending sound.

An Island Grows

by **Lola M. Schaefer** • illustrated by **Cathie Felstead**

▸ **Set a Purpose**

Find out how an **island** forms in the **ocean**.

Deep, deep ***beneath*** *the sea...*

Stone breaks.

Water **quakes**.

Magma glows.

Volcano blows.

Lava flows and flows and flows.

An **island** grows.

beneath *under*
quakes shakes
sheer very tall and straight
Weather batters. Wind and rain hit the rocks.
shatters breaks into tiny pieces

Waves **pound**.
Sands mound.

Winds sow
seeds that blow.

pound hit hard
Sands mound. The sand piles up in hills.
Winds sow Winds help to plant

tower grow tall
Vines Plants
thrive live

Before You Continue

1. **Draw Conclusions** Reread the text that describes how an **island** forms. What can you conclude about how long it takes?
2. **Rhyme** Look for words that rhyme. Find two examples.

Predict

What do you think will happen next on the **island**?

Sailors **spot**.
Maps plot.

Ships **dock**.
Traders **flock**.

spot see something

Maps plot. People use maps to plan their course.

dock stop and stay

flock come in great numbers

Settlers stay.
Children play.

Workers build.
Soil is tilled.

Settlers People looking for a new home
Soil is tilled. People prepare the soil for planting.

Markets sell.
Merchants yell.

"Fresh fish!"
"Pepper dish!"

"Ripe fruit!"
"Spicy **root**!"

Merchants Sellers
root vegetable

Bells ring.

Voices sing.

Drums play.

Dancers **sway**.

sway move from side to side

Before You Continue

1. **Confirm Prediction** Who comes to the **island**? Was your prediction right?
2. **Visualize** Reread the text on this page. What pictures and sounds do the words make in your mind?

Predict
What will happen if another **volcano erupts** under the **ocean**?

Busy **island** in the sea where
only water used to be.

Then, one day, not far away,
deep beneath the sea,

a **volcano** blows,
and **lava flows**.

Another **island** grows. ❖

Before You Continue

1. **Confirm Prediction** Did you think the **volcano erupting** would make another **island**? Why or why not?
2. **Rhythm** Read the text again. Clap out the poem's rhythm.

PART 1 Think and Respond

Key Words	
core	lava
create	magma
develop	ocean
erupt	pressure
flow	rock
force	volcano
island	

Talk About It

1. Think about the characteristics of a **narrative poem**. Why is the selection a narrative poem?

   The selection is a narrative poem because ____.

2. Think about the new **island** that **developed**. Will it be the same as the first one? **Tell a story** about what happens.

   First, ____. Then, ____. Finally ____.

3. When the first island formed, people came to live on it. What conclusion can you draw about these people?

   People who settle on a new island are probably ____ and ____. They ____.

Write About It

The selection tells about different things settlers do, such as **create** farms, build houses, and sell food. If you lived on the island, what job would you like? Why would you like that job? Use **Key Words** in your answers.

If I lived on the island, I would ____.
I would like that job because ____.

Reread and Retell

Imagery

"An Island Grows" tells the story of how an **island** comes to be. With a partner, discuss how word pictures help tell the story. Then make an imagery chart for the poem. Write words for each category that tell how things look, sound, smell, taste, or feel.

Imagery Chart

Volcano	Land	Plants	Animals	People
Stone breaks. Water quakes.				

With your partner, use your completed chart to describe how an island grows. Use the sentence frames and **Key Words**. Record your description.

These lines tell about volcanoes: ______ .
These lines tell about land: ______ .

Fluency

Practice reading with intonation. Rate your reading.

Talk Together

How can a volcanic eruption change Earth? Draw a picture. Add a caption with **Key Words**. Explain your drawing to your classmates.

PART 1 Word Work

Greek and Latin Roots

Some English words contain **Greek and Latin roots**. A root is a word part that has meaning, but a root is not a word on its own.

If you know the meaning of a word's root, it can help you figure out the meaning of the word.

Greek and Latin Roots Chart

Origin	Root	Meaning	Example
Greek	*geo*	Earth	**geology:** the study of Earth's history and structure
Latin	*volcan*	a god of fire	**volcano:** a mountain that hot melted rock can come out of
	rupt	to break	**erupt:** to explode or shoot out

Try It Together

Read each item. Choose the best answer.

1. Which word has something to do with Earth?

A germ
B gallon
C legend
D geography

2. Which word has something to do with an opening or a crack?

A rush
B melt
C erase
D rupture

Making Connections Read a photo essay to see just how dangerous **volcanoes** can be.

Genre A **photo essay** is nonfiction. It uses photographs and text to give information.

Volcano Views

with photographs by **Carsten Peter** and text by **Chris Beem**

Carsten Peter is an award-winning photographer. He takes pictures in some of the most dangerous places on Earth. Look at these amazing photographs. To take the pictures, Peter had to get very close to **active volcanoes**!

Carsten Peter by an active volcano

Volcano Views Pictures of Volcanoes
active erupting

Before You Continue

1. **Draw Conclusions** What kind of person is Carsten Peter? How do you know?
2. **Use Text Features** What can you learn about an active volcano from the photograph?

Fiery Forces

What makes a volcano erupt? The **process** starts when magma, or hot liquid rock, collects under **Earth's crust**. When enough pressure builds up, the magma **bursts** up through the ground. This is like blowing too much air into a balloon. What happens? The balloon pops!

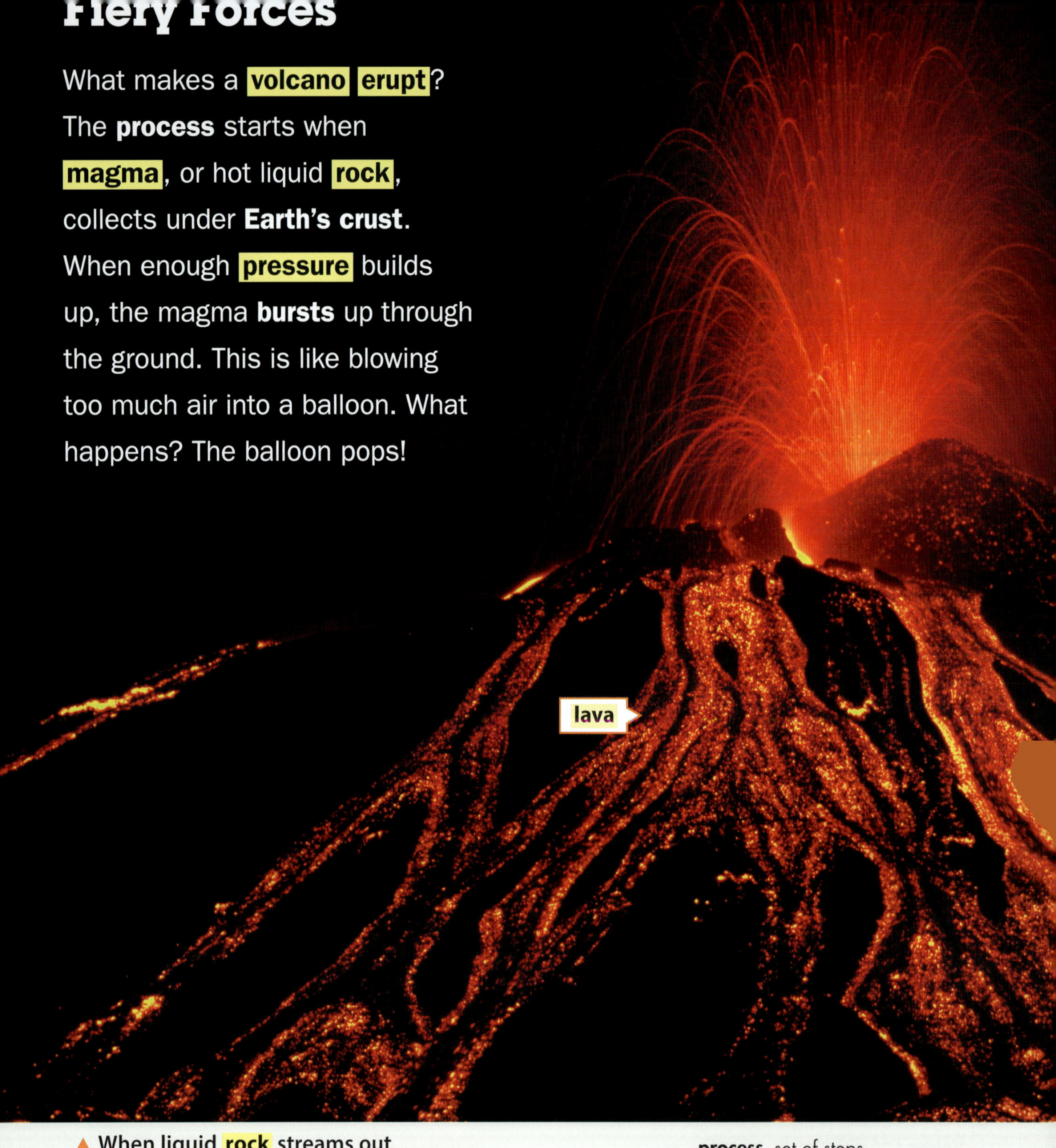

When liquid rock streams out of a volcano, it is called lava.

process set of steps
Earth's crust the surface of Earth
bursts pushes

Different things happen when volcanoes erupt. Some eruptions force gases, rock, and smoke out of the **crater**. Other eruptions only **release** smoke. In some volcanoes, lava just **oozes** out of the volcano's top. Then the lava flows like a river down its sides.

▲ A Carsten Peter photo of rock exploding from a crater.

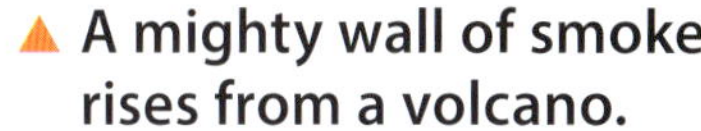

▲ A mighty wall of smoke rises from a volcano.

crater top of the volcano
release let out
oozes flows slowly

Before You Continue

1. **Use Text Features** Read the caption on page 176. How would you describe lava?
2. **Evaluate** Choose one type of eruption explained on this page. Describe the damage it might do.

Rivers of Heat

Lava is HOT. When it first **escapes from** a **volcano**, its temperature is between **1,300 and 2,200 degrees Fahrenheit**! As lava moves down a mountainside, it glows bright orange, like a fiery sunset. Thick lava may **inch along**, but thin lava can **flow** more quickly.

▲ Peter's photographs capture the heat of **lava**.

escapes from leaves
1,300 to 2,200 degrees Fahrenheit about 700 to 1,200 degrees Celsius
inch along move very slowly

A Close-Up Look

Red-hot **lava**. Clouds of smoke and gas. Flying **rocks**. All of these things make active **volcanoes** **extremely** dangerous. Most people would run away from these **forces** of nature. Carsten Peter runs toward them. Thanks to his amazing photos, we can **get a close-up glimpse of** volcanoes in action. ❖

▲ This photograph shows a special suit that can help keep out the heat.

extremely very, very
get a close-up glimpse of clearly see

Before You Continue

1. **Details** What did you learn about **lava**? Give at least two details from the text.
2. **Imagery** Which words on page 178 help you form a mental picture of lava?

PART 1 **Respond and Extend**

Compare Texts

Key Words	
core	lava
create	magma
develop	ocean
erupt	pressure
flow	rock
force	volcano
island	

"An Island Grows" is a literary text, and "Volcano Views" is an informational text. The selections are different, but they have some similar ideas.

What does each selection tell about **volcanoes**? Complete a comparison chart with a partner. Find evidence in the selections that supports what you write on your chart.

Comparison Chart

"An Island Grows"	"Volcano Views"
Tells about volcanoes under the sea	Tells about a man who photographs volcanoes
Tells about magma and lava	Tells about magma and lava

Talk Together

What **forces** can change Earth? Think about both selections. What did you learn in one selection that you did not learn in the other? Use **Key Words** to discuss your ideas.

Adverbs

Adverbs usually tell more about a verb.

Grammar Rules Adverbs

• Use an **adverb** to tell how, where, or when something happens.	Islands grow **slowly**. (how) Rocks are **everywhere**. (where) Ships sail by **today**. (when)
• For some adverbs, add **-er** to compare two actions. Add **-est** to compare three or more actions.	Thin lava flows fast**er** than thick lava. This lava flows the fast**est** of all.
• If an adverb ends in **-ly**, use **more** or **less** to compare two actions. Use **the most** or **the least** to compare three or more actions.	Li swims **more** quick**ly** than Tom. Tom swims **less** quick**ly** than Li. Uma swims **the most** quick**ly** of all. I swim **the least** quick**ly** of all.

Read Adverbs

Read these sentences with a partner. Find two adverbs.

Waves pound the shore loudly. Winds blow the sand around.

Write Adverbs 

Write three sentences about an island. Use at least two adverbs. Read your sentences to your partner.

Language Frames

I think ______.

I believe ______.

In my opinion, ______.

Express Opinions and Ideas

Listen to Larry and Nia's song. Then use **Language Frames** to express your opinions and ideas about forces of nature.

Here's What I Think

Song

Larry:
I think it is important
That we understand—
Earthquakes will occur,
And they will shake the land.

Nia:
I believe most people
Needn't be too scared.
But, in my opinion,
We must be prepared.

Tune: "Au Clair de la Lune"

How to Prepare for an Earthquake

Make an Emergency Kit
- water
- radio
- food
- money
- flashlight
- first-aid kit
- batteries
- clothing

Science Vocabulary

Key Words

Key Words
earthquake
plate
shore
tsunami
wave

Look at this diagram. Use **Key Words** and other words to talk about the picture. What happens because of an underwater **earthquake**?

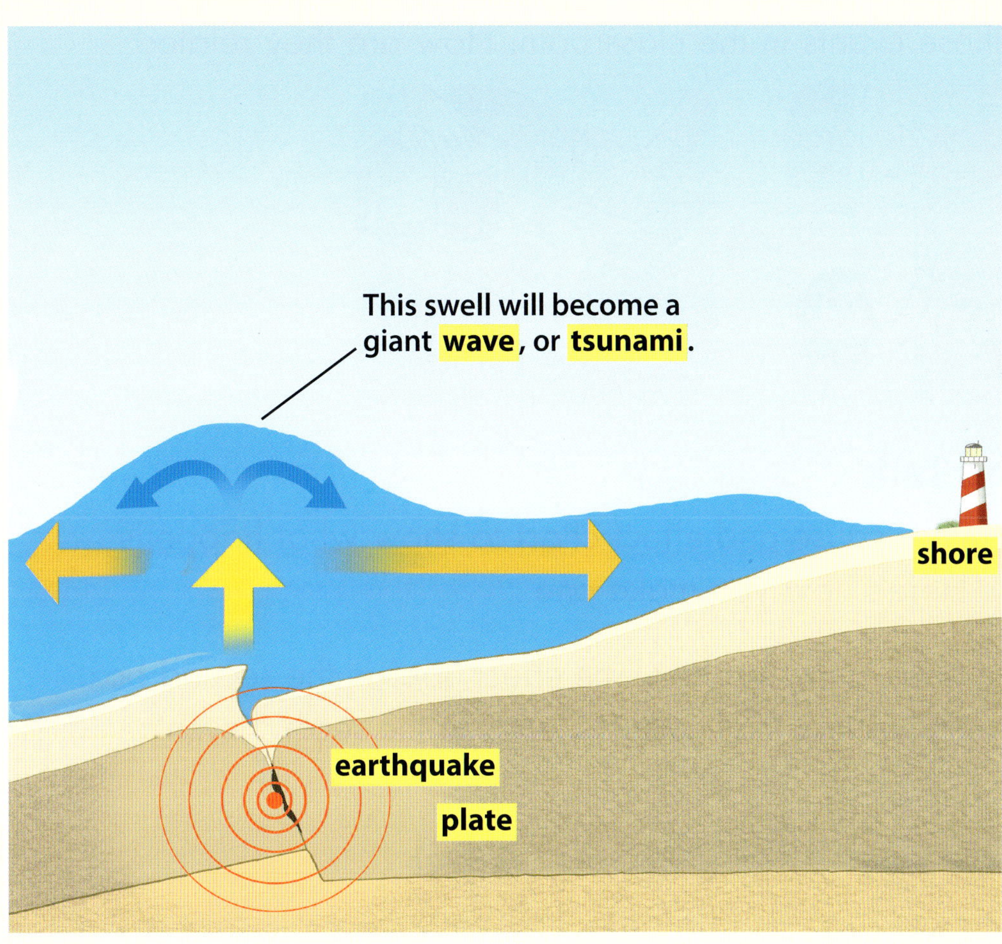

Talk Together

What forces under the sea can change Earth? How should you prepare for a disaster near the ocean? Talk to a partner. Express your opinions and ideas. Use **Language Frames** from page 182 and **Key Words**.

Cause and Effect

The **cause** is why something happens. The **effect** is what happens. Causes and effects help you understand how events are related.

Look at these events in the classroom. How are they related?

Map and Talk

You can use a cause-and-effect chart to show what happens and why. Here's how you make one.

The cause goes in the first box. The effect goes in the second box. The arrow shows that the first event leads to the second event.

Cause-and-Effect Chart

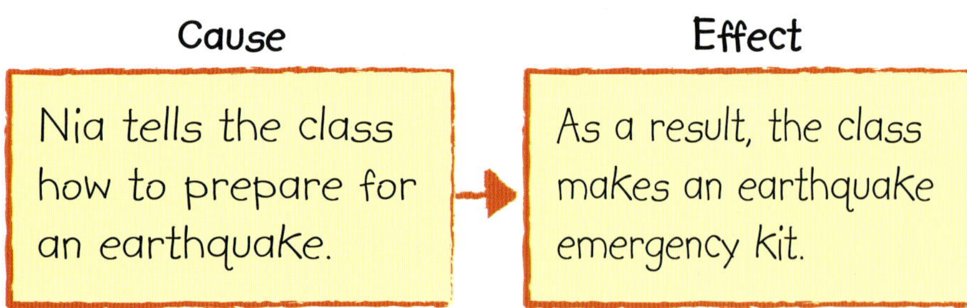

Talk Together

Look back at the diagram on page 183. Make a cause-and-effect chart that shows what you think will happen. Share your chart with a partner.

Academic Vocabulary

More Key Words

Use these words to talk about "Selvakumar Knew Better" and "Tsunami."

power
noun

If something has **power**, it is strong. Strong waves have the **power** to destroy a building.

rescue
verb

When you **rescue** someone, you save them. A dog helps to **rescue** someone.

sense
verb

When you **sense** something, you know it without being told. A cat can **sense** danger.

signal
noun

A **signal** is something that tells you what to do. The green light is a **signal** to walk.

warn
verb

To **warn** people is to tell them that something bad may happen. She **warns** people to stop.

Talk Together

With a partner, take turns telling a story with the **Key Words**.

The storm has a lot of power!

Mom warned us to stay inside.

PART 2 **Reading Strategy**

Learn to Form Generalizations

Look at the photo. Notice the people. Would most people act like that if they saw huge **waves**? **Form a generalization**, or decide what most people would do.

A **generalization** is a statement that applies to many situations. When you read, you **form generalizations**, too.

How to Form Generalizations

1. Pay attention to the important ideas in the text.
2. Think about the ideas. How are they like things you know from your own life?
3. Make a statement that seems true for both the text and what you know.

I read ______.

I know ______.

I think that most ______.

Talk Together

Read Nia's fact sheet. Read the sample generalization. Then use **Language Frames** to make generalizations as you read. Tell a partner about them.

Language Frames

- I read ______ .
- I know ______ .
- I think that most ______ .

Fact Sheet

Three Tsunamis

This fact sheet will give you an idea of a **tsunami's** **power**. People were not **warned** in time to escape these disasters. There were no warning **signals**. People did not **sense** the tsunamis coming. Many people were **rescued**, but many others lost their lives.

Sample Generalization

"I read that people did not sense the tsunamis. I know about other tsunamis that people did not know were coming. I think that most people cannot tell that a tsunami is coming."

Earthquake Energy Scale
4.0 = Light 5.0 = Strong 7.0 = Major 8.0 = Great 9.0 = Greater 10.0 = Greatest

Time, Place, Size	Cause	Effect
2004 Indian Ocean; Waves up to 50 feet	9.0 undersea earthquake	Flooded the coastlines of 12 countries; swept away islands and villages
1998 Papua, New Guinea; Waves up to 40 feet	Undersea landslide created by 7.1 undersea earthquake	Destroyed at least two villages
1964 Alaska and northwestern United States; Waves up to 220 feet	9.2 undersea earthquake	Caused hundreds of miles of coastal damage from Alaska to Northern California

◀ = A good place to form a generalization

PART 2 **Phonics Focus**

Syllable Pattern: Consonant + *-le, -al, -el*

marble

hospital

label

Listen and Learn

Listen to the ending syllables of the words in the box. Then sort the words by how that syllable is spelled.

metal	circle	camel	medal	jungle
petal	bagel	puzzle	label	

-le	**-al**	**-el**
______	______	______
______	______	______
______	______	______

Complete each sentence with a word from the lists above.

1. You can ride on a ______.
2. My bike is made of ______.
3. Many animals live in the ______.

Talk Together

Listen and read. Find the words with the consonant plus *-le*, *-al*, or *-el* pattern.

Over to You

Early Warning Systems

In my opinion, early warning systems are important. It's simple. I believe that just a few minutes can save lives. For example, most injuries in an earthquake are from things falling. An earthquake makes the ground move. Flat or level ground breaks up. Buildings shake. Things fall. Walls fall. Buildings fall. A signal can warn people that an earthquake is coming. Then they can get to safe places. There are machines that sense movement in the earth. Sometimes they are little movements. Sometimes they are big movements. The machines can predict earthquakes. They can warn people.

A tsunami is caused by an underwater earthquake. It is made up of huge waves. The waves hit the shore. A tsunami is dangerous. Tsunamis destroy buildings. They injure or kill people. They cause great floods. Tsunami warning signals let local people know a tsunami is coming. It can warn people hours before the waves come. Then people can get to safe places.

Warning signals work. They help people. They save lives.

Work with a partner.

Point to words that end with a consonant + *-le*, *-al*, or *-el*. Have your partner read them. Count the syllables in the words you find.

Practice reading words that end with a consonant + *-le*, *-al*, or *-el* by reading "Early Warning Systems" with a partner.

Read Historical Fiction

Genre

Historical fiction is a made-up story based on real events and people from the past.

Dialogue

Dialogue is what characters say to one another in a story. Writers use quotation marks to show dialogue.

> Selvakumar whined, and Mama said, "Hush." Selvakumar barked, and Dinakaran complained, "Quiet, I'm trying to concentrate."

Quotation marks show a character's exact words.

Selvakumar Knew Better

by Virginia Kroll

illustrated by Xiaojun Li

Set a Purpose
Find out what a dog **senses** that his human family does not.

The December day in south India **dawned** like any other, **kissed by the golden sun.** Papa came back with his boat full of fish. Mama made breakfast for seven-year-old Dinakaran and his two little brothers. That day seemed like any other day, but Selvakumar **knew better**.

Selvakumar felt a **rumbling** in his belly. His legs **were restless**, and his scruffy yellow fur stood on end. His ears perked up, listening for the sound that had already started.

dawned started
kissed by the golden sun with bright sunshine
knew better thought something else
rumbling shaking
were restless felt strange

His family didn't **notice**. Papa was busy unloading his **catch**, and Mama was hanging her laundry. Dinakaran was finishing his homework, while the younger boys ran around the yard.

Selvakumar **whined**, and Mama said, "Hush." Selvakumar barked, and Dinakaran complained, "Quiet, I'm trying to **concentrate**."

Suddenly, a strange roaring sound began. Mama thought that a thunderstorm was coming, but Dinakaran and his brothers thought it was an extra-loud train. Papa ran to a nearby building's roof to **investigate**.

notice see
catch fish
whined made a crying sound
concentrate think
investigate find out what was happening

But Selvakumar knew better. The **vibrations** traveled up his padded paws. His skin prickled with fearful goose bumps from his black nose to his tufted tail. He wanted to run, but he **dared not** leave his family. Sometimes humans didn't **realize**.

Why were they waiting? Didn't they know that a mighty **earthquake** had rumbled under the ocean and would soon bring raging **waves** onto the **shore**?

And then Papa shouted **desperately** from the rooftop, "**Tsunami**! Run!"

vibrations shaking of the ground
dared not did not want to
realize know what was happening
desperately with fear

Mama screamed, "Sons, come on!" She grabbed a little one under each arm. "Dinakaran, run! You're **swift** and strong. Follow me up the hill. Fast!"

But the roar had gotten louder, cutting off her words. All that Dinakaran had heard was, "Run!" And he ran back to his family's house close to the shore, where he thought he would be safe.

But Selvakumar knew better. He barked and howled, but the sound of **approaching waves drowned out** his voice, too.

swift fast

approaching waves drowned out the tsunami made it hard to hear

Before You Continue

1. **Form Generalizations** Based on the text and what you know, what can you say about Selvakumar? What kind of dog is he?
2. **Cause/Effect** Why does Dinakaran run home instead of up the hill?

Predict

What will Selvakumar do to help Dinakaran?

Selvakumar **nipped at Dinakaran's heels**, but the boy wouldn't **budge**. "Go." Dinakaran **shooed** the dog away, but Selvakumar knew better and would not give up. He grabbed Dinakaran's shirt in his teeth. He pulled and tugged until his teeth hurt. With all his strength, he dragged Dinakaran back outside and bumped him from behind. Finally, the boy understood.

nipped at Dinakaran's heels gently bit the boy's feet

budge move

shooed pushed

Selvakumar ran toward the hill, looking back to make sure Dinakaran was following. They raced uphill as the **enormous** wall of water chased them. The **tsunami** roared louder than five thunderstorms and ten trains put together.

Selvakumar and Dinakaran didn't stop running until they reached the upper road. Their sides **ached**, and their breaths felt like hot coals burning in their chests.

enormous huge
ached hurt

Dinakaran wanted to stop, but Selvakumar knew better. He **nudged** Dinakaran's hand, and together they **continued** higher up the hill.

Finally, they turned and looked down toward the **shore**. They both blinked their eyes **in disbelief**.

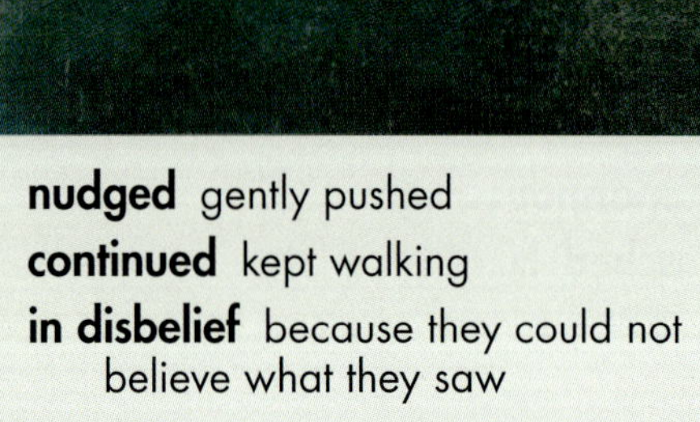

nudged gently pushed

continued kept walking

in disbelief because they could not believe what they saw

The **wave** had swallowed everything. It had **snapped** trees as if they were **brittle** little sticks. It had **collapsed** all the houses flat as if they'd been birds' nests.

snapped broken
brittle dry
collapsed smashed

Before You Continue

1. **Confirm Prediction** Did you predict what Selvakumar would do? Explain.
2. **Make Inferences** Why do you think Dinakaran was in disbelief when he looked at his village?

Predict
What will happen next to Selvakumar and Dinakaran?

In the distance, Selvakumar and Dinakaran heard Mama's voice. "Dinakaran," she **wailed** over and over. "My **firstborn** son is lost!" They walked toward the sound and found her rocking back and forth as her younger sons **sobbed** beside her.

Selvakumar **yipped and bounded** toward her, and Mama's head **snapped up**. She wiped her tears and stared at Dinakaran. "My precious son, you're alive!" she whispered. Dinakaran rushed into her arms, and she covered him in grateful kisses.

wailed cried
firstborn oldest
sobbed cried loudly
yipped and bounded barked and ran
snapped up looked up quickly

"I-I went to th-the house, Mama. I-I thought I'd be sa-safe. B-but Sel-Selvakumar knew better," he **sputtered** as his tears mixed with Mama's. He told her about what the dog had done.

Mama let go of Dinakaran and hugged Selvakumar hard. Selvakumar greeted the smaller boys with face licks.

Papa joined them after the **tsunami** disappeared, and when he heard the story, he sobbed into Selvakumar's fur, too. Then they were all a mother-father-brothers-dog **thankful heap** of hugging.

sputtered said excitedly
thankful heap happy group

Later, the other **survivors** of the village gathered in a **temporary shelter**. They heard about many, many lives that had been lost.

As Dinakaran and Selvakumar rested, they heard the grownups talking.

"We'll never **recover**," moaned one man.

"We've lost absolutely everything," someone else said.

But Selvakumar felt the regular rhythm of Dinakaran's chest rising and falling under his chin. Then he heard Dinakaran's little brothers nearby. He smelled the familiar scents of Papa and Mama.

And Selvakumar knew better. ❖

survivors people who escaped the tsunami

temporary shelter safe place

recover fix everything; have the same things we used to

Before You Continue

1. **Confirm Prediction** What happened to Selvakumar and Dinakaran? Was your prediction correct?
2. **Dialogue** How does the dialogue on page 201 show exactly how Dinakaran is feeling?

Meet the Illustrator

Xiaojun Li

"Like many people around the world, the tsunami disaster shocked me and my family," says Xiaojun Li. After reading the story of *Selvakumar Knew Better*, Mr. Li researched images of the tsunami. "When I felt confident that I could express the powerful emotions felt by the victims, I began the illustrations."

Mr. Li used photographs to create the sketches of Dinakaran, his mother, and the setting.

▲ **Xiaojun Li at his home studio**

▲ **Dinakaran, his mother, and Selvakumar**

Artist's Craft

Mr. Li uses details in his art to show characters' emotions. Choose a picture of one of the characters in the story. Tell what the character is feeling or thinking. How does Mr. Li's art show this?

PART 2

Think and Respond

Key Words	
earthquake	shore
plate	signal
power	tsunami
rescue	warn
sense	wave

Talk About It

1. How do you know that the story is **historical fiction**?

   I know that it is historical fiction because _____.

2. Dinakaran's family lives near the **shore**. What would you tell them if they asked whether they should rebuild their home there? **Express opinions and ideas** about it.

   I think _____. In my opinion, _____. But _____.

3. Does the story have a first-person or a third-person narrator? How would the story be different if Dinakaran were the narrator?

   The narrator is _____. If Dinakaran were the narrator, _____.

Write About It

What do you think about Selvakumar's actions? What would you say to him if he could understand you? Write three sentences. Use **Key Words** to help explain your thoughts.

Selvakumar, I think you _____. You _____.

Reread and Summarize

Cause and Effect

Make a cause-and-effect chart for "Selvakumar Knew Better."

Cause-and-Effect Chart

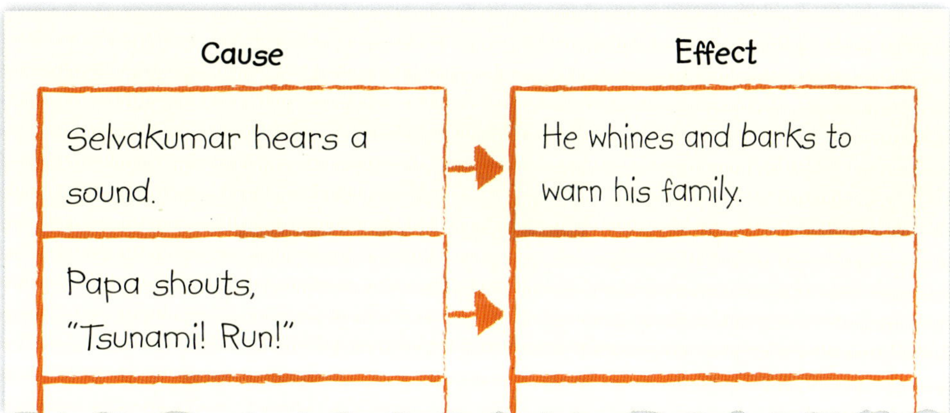

Cause		Effect
Selvakumar hears a sound.	→	He whines and barks to warn his family.
Papa shouts, "Tsunami! Run!"	→	

Look at the sequence of events in the chart. With a partner, discuss how each event influences a future event. Then use your chart to summarize the plot's main events. Use **Key Words**. Record your summary.

Fluency

Practice reading with expression. Rate your reading.

Talk Together

How can a **tsunami** change Earth? What might Dinakaran say to visitors? Write dialogue with **Key Words**. Read your dialogue with your partner.

PART 2 Word Work

Compound Words

A **compound word** is made up of two smaller words. To figure out what a compound word means, look at the smaller words.

earth: "land," "ground"
quake: "shake"
earth + quake = **earthquake**

Meaning: a sudden shaking of the ground

sea: "ocean"
shore: "land next to water"
sea + shore = **seashore**

Meaning: land next to the sea or ocean

Try It Together

Read the sentences. Then answer the questions.

As we hike up the volcano, we leave a trail of footprints. When we reach the mountaintop, we look down into a huge crater.

1. What do you think footprints means?

A hiking shoes
B written signs
C food wrappings
D marks left by shoes or feet

2. What do you think mountaintop means?

A the end of a trail
B a fence around a crater
C a view from a mountain
D the highest part of a mountain

Making Connections Read this article to learn more about **tsunamis**.

Genre An **online article** is an article that is on the Internet.

A **tsunami** is a **series** of huge **waves**. **A disturbance** under the sea, such as an **earthquake** or volcanic eruption, causes the waves.

series group
A disturbance An important event

Before You Continue

1. **Main Idea** What is a tsunami?
2. **Cause/Effect** What causes a tsunami?

Tsunami

https://eltngl.com/reachhigherseries

How a Tsunami Forms

During an event under the water, such as an **earthquake**, a lot of energy is produced. That strong force pushes upward and out. It makes **waves** move in all directions. When waves reach **shallow water** they grow higher. They can reach as high as 100 feet! These powerful waves then crash onto the **shore**. They can **cause heavy damage**.

A Tsunami Forms Under Water

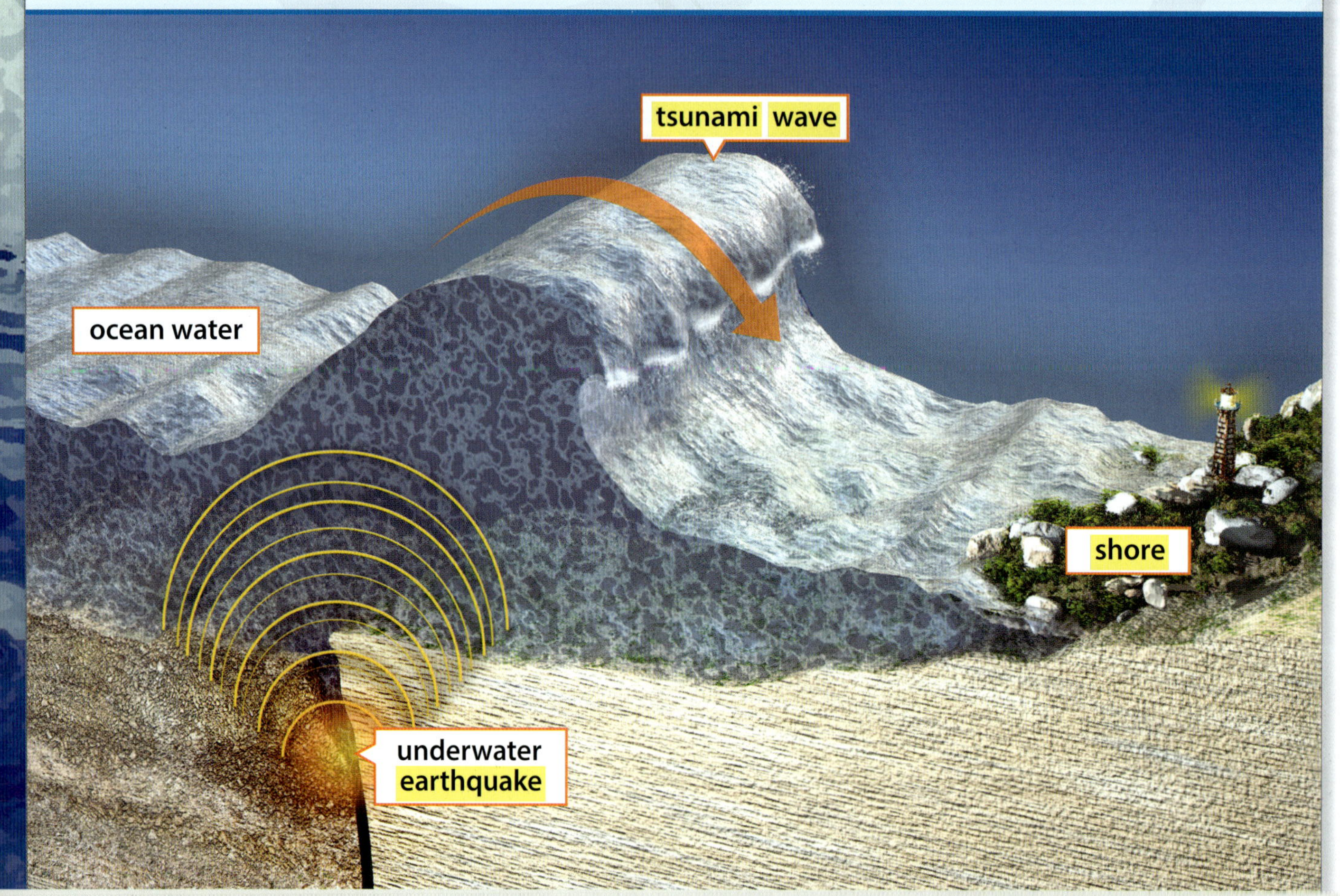

shallow water places in the ocean where the water is not as deep

cause heavy damage hurt many people and ruin things

Areas at Risk

Hawaii is at the greatest risk for a **tsunami**. The American state gets about one each year. It gets a damaging tsunami every seven years. Alaska is also at high risk. California, Oregon, and Washington **experience** a damaging tsunami about once every 18 years.

In 1946, a tsunami crashed into Hilo, Hawaii. The **waves** were as high as a three-story building.

In 1964, an **earthquake** shook the state of Alaska. It caused a tsunami along parts of the Washington, Oregon, and California **shore**. The waves were 10 to 20 feet high.

Learn about tsunami warning centers.

Areas at Risk of Tsunamis in the U.S.A.

▲ Tsunami damage in Alaska, 1964

Areas at Risk Places in Danger from Tsunamis
experience have

▶ Before You Continue

1. **Form Generalizations** Look at the map. Think about the places that are at high risk of **tsunamis**. In what ways are they all alike?
2. **Cause/Effect** What can happen if a tsunami hits the **shore**?

Tracking a Tsunami

https://eltngl.com/reachhigherseries

Tracking a Tsunami

Tsunami Warning Centers

In the United States, there are two **tsunami** warning centers. They **monitor** events that could cause a tsunami. The centers are located in Hawaii and Alaska.

In the warning centers, people **track** information about **wave sizes and water pressure**. The information comes from **devices** in the ocean. People use the information to predict if a tsunami is likely to happen.

▲ The tsunami warning center in Hawaii

monitor watch for
track look for changes in
wave sizes and water pressure changes in ocean water
devices machines

Early Warnings

Scientists place **recorders** on the ocean floor. They are placed in areas that have a history of disturbances that cause **tsunamis**. The recorders collect information and send it to **buoys**. The buoys then send all the information back to the warning centers **by satellite**.

Tsunamis can be deadly. So being able to **warn** people about a tsunami before it reaches **shore** can save a lot of lives. ❖

How a Buoy System Works

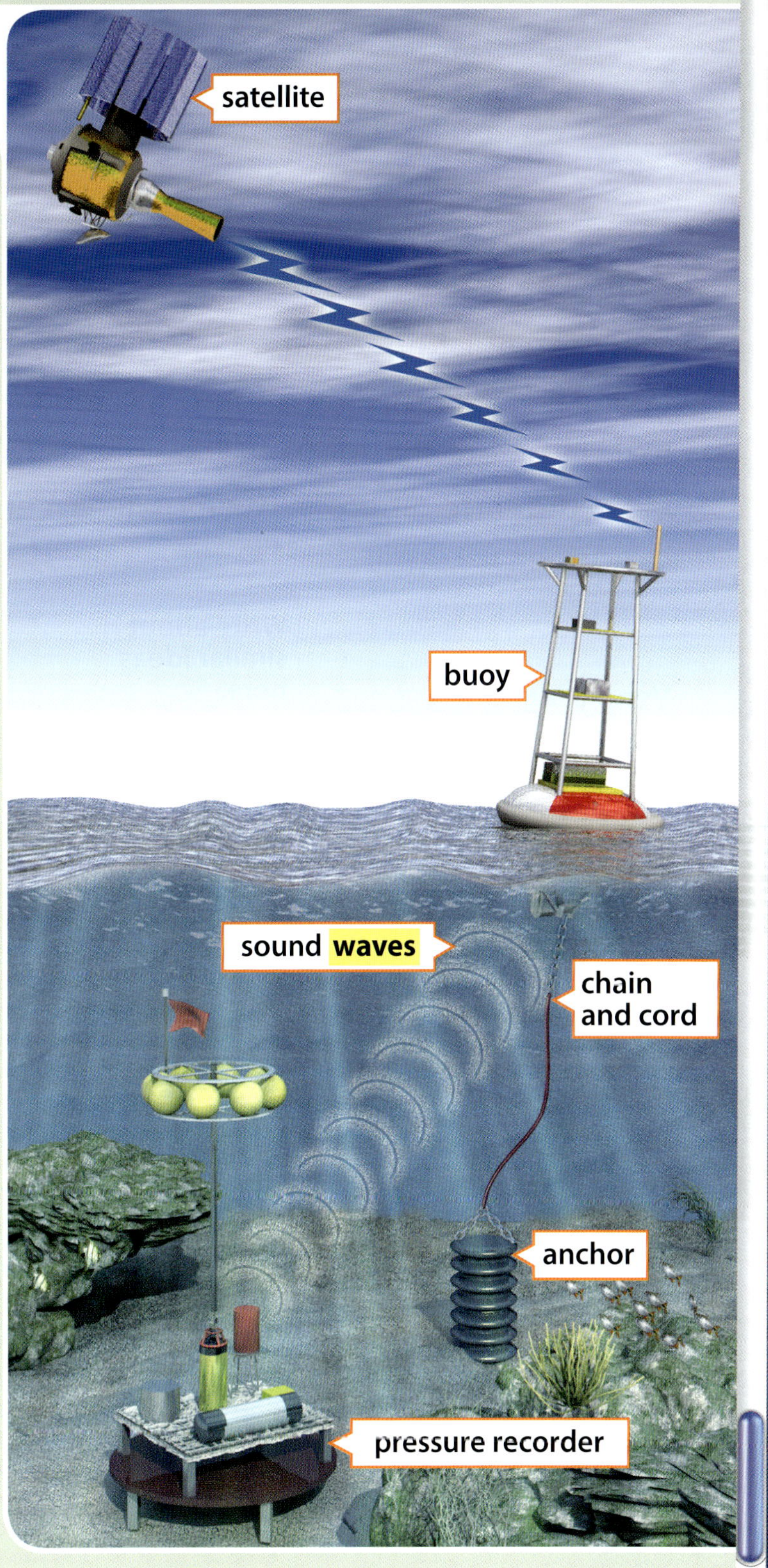

recorders machines that measure changes in ocean water

buoys objects that float on top of the water

by satellite in messages

▸ Before You Continue

1. **Use Text Features** Use the diagram to explain how a buoy system works.
2. **Make Inferences** What information might the warning center include in its warning?

PART 2 Respond and Extend

Key Words	
earthquake	shore
plate	signal
power	tsunami
rescue	warn
sense	wave

Compare Texts

"Selvakumar Knew Better" is a literary text, and "Tsunami" is an informational text. How are the ideas in the selections similar, or the same? How are they different? Complete a Venn diagram with a partner.

Venn Diagram

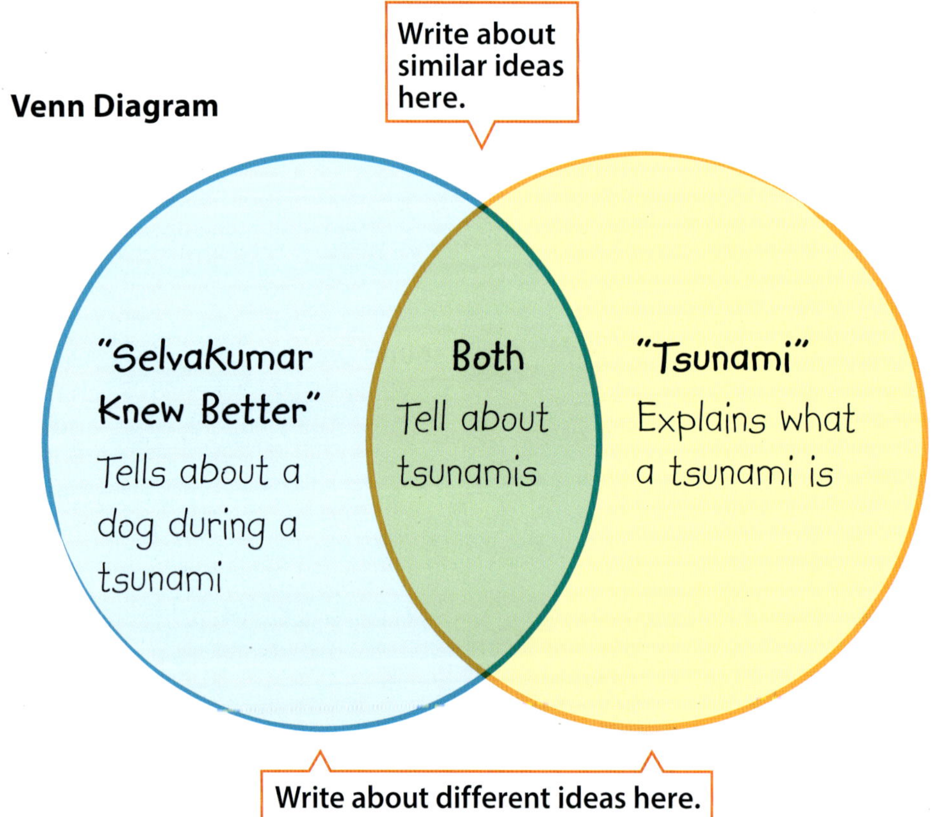

Talk Together

What forces in the ocean can change Earth? Think about the story and the online article. Use **Key Words** in your discussion.

Grammar

Prepositional Phrases

A preposition can tell where, show direction, show time, or add details. A **prepositional phrase** starts with a preposition and ends with a noun or pronoun. Use prepositional phrases to:

Grammar Rules **Prepositional Phrases**

	Prepositional Phrase in a Sentence
• show where something is	Our village is **by the ocean**.
• show direction	I climbed **up the mountain**.
• show time	**After the tsunami**, we went home.
• add details	Birds fly **around us**. Hot sand is **under our feet**.

Read Prepositional Phrases

Read this passage from "Selvakumar Knew Better." Can you find two prepositional phrases?

> She grabbed a little one under each arm. "Dinakaran, run! You're swift and strong. Follow me up the hill. Fast!"

Write Prepositional Phrases 

Write a caption for the picture on page 197. Use a prepositional phrase. Share your caption with a partner.

Writing Project

Write Like a Researcher

Write a Research Report 

Write a report about a force of nature that can change Earth. Combine your report with those of your classmates to create a science book or a multimedia show.

Study a Model

When you write a research report, you gather information from several sources. You organize the facts that you find. Then you present the facts in a way that is all your own.

Earthquake!

by Zachary Wilkes

The ground shakes. Windows break. Roads crack. It's an earthquake!

There are between 2,000 and 3,000 earthquakes in the United States of America every year. Most of them are too small to feel. Bigger ones can destroy cities. Why can't we protect ourselves better from these disasters?

First, it's important to know what causes earthquakes. Earth is actually made up of layers. The top layer is called the crust. The crust is formed by large slabs of rock, called plates. These plates fit together like pieces of a puzzle.

The title and introduction tell what the report is about. The introduction gets the reader's attention.

The **focus** of the report is clear.

Each paragraph has a **topic sentence** that tells the main idea of the paragraph.

Facts and details support each topic sentence.

The writing is well-organized and smooth. Each idea flows into the next idea.

Sometimes the plates move and begin pushing against each other. This causes pressure along the edges of the plates. If the pressure builds up too much, then the plates suddenly bump past each other. The energy this releases makes the ground shake, and we feel an earthquake.

If we know what causes earthquakes, why can't we predict them? First of all, no one knows when the plates in Earth's crust will move. The closest we can come to guessing that is

Sources

"Earthquake." *World Book Encyclopedia*. 2009. 33–39. Print.

Earthquake Hazards Program. U.S. Geological Survey, 11 Feb. 2010. Web. 12 Feb. 2010. <http://earthquake.usgs.gov/learn/kids/>

Walker, Sally M. *Earthquakes.* Minneapolis, Minnesota: Carolrhoda Books, 2008. Print.

The sources that are used for the report are listed on a final page.

Writing Project, continued

Prewrite

1. **Choose a Topic** What did you read about in the unit that interests you? What other forces of nature would you like to learn about?

   Share your ideas with a partner. Narrow your topic. Choose one that you can find sources for and cover well in a short report.

2. **List Your Research Questions** What do you already know about your topic? What do you need to find out? With your partner, think of questions to guide you as you do your research.

   Research Questions

   - What causes earthquakes?
   - Where do earthquakes happen?
   - What is it like to be in an earthquake?
   - Can earthquakes be predicted?

3. **Create a Research Plan** A research plan lists your questions. It also lists your ideas for how to answer them.

   Different sources can help you with different kinds of questions. Books, magazine articles, and websites are all examples of sources that can help you with research.

Gather Information

1. **Identify Sources** To find books that would be good sources for your topic, skim tables of contents, headings, and pictures. To see if websites are helpful, check menus on the home page.

   Make sure every source is up to date. Also make sure each one comes from a group or person who is an expert in the area.

2. **Create Source Cards** Keep track of your sources on cards.

   Source Card for a Book

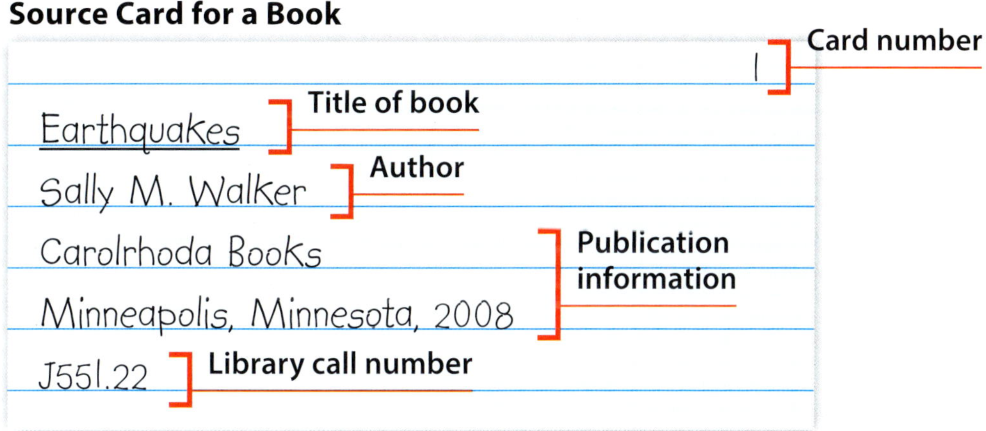

3. **Make Note Cards** Create note cards to record important words, phrases, and ideas that you find as you research.

   Note Card

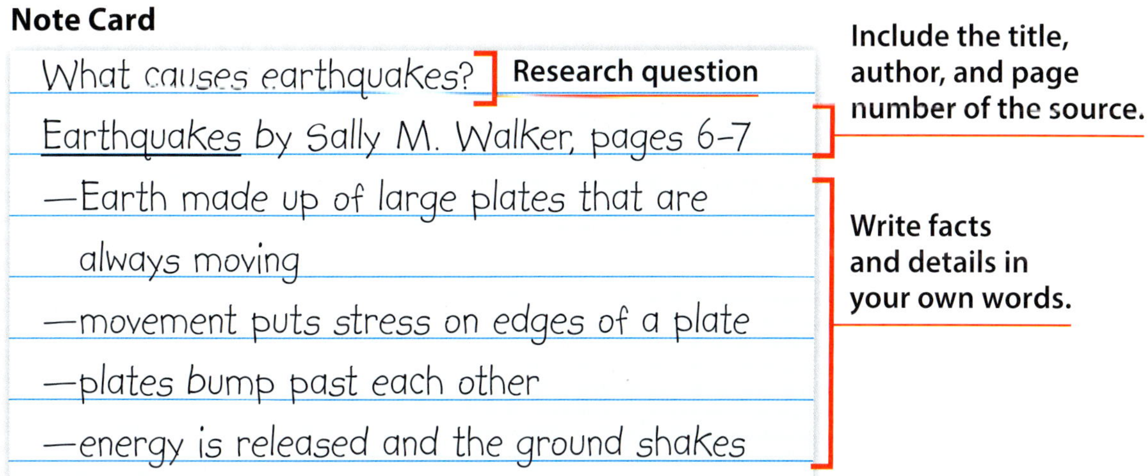

Get Organized

1. **Arrange Your Cards** Put your cards in an order that makes sense. Use the research question on each card to help you. Put cards with similar research questions in the same group.
2. **Organize Your Information** Use a main idea and details diagram to help you organize your information. Each research question, or group of similar research questions, can become a main idea. Put the details for those questions under the main idea.

Main Idea and Details Diagram

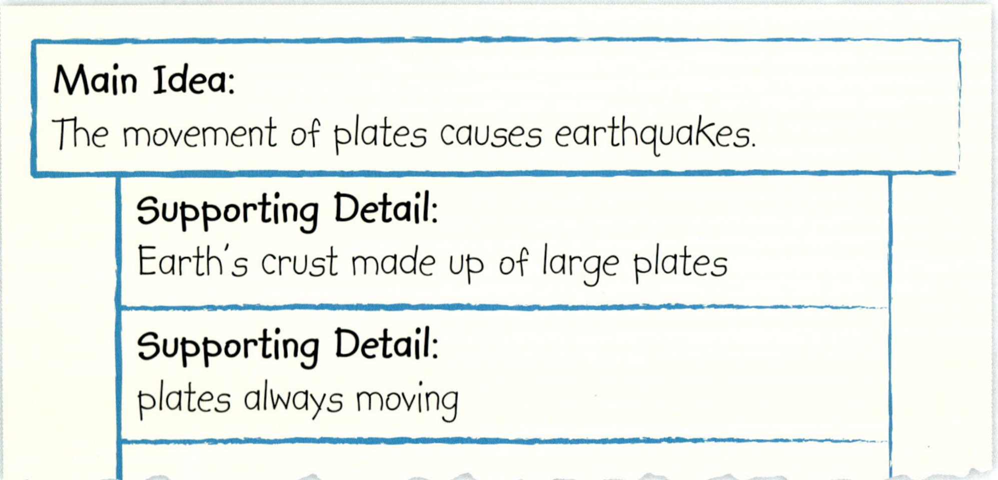

Draft

Use your diagram to guide you as you write a draft. Put all the information in your own words. Never use words directly from the source. To use someone else's words is to plagiarize, which is a type of stealing.

Revise

1. **Read, Retell, Respond** Read your draft aloud to a partner. Your partner listens and summarizes the main points of the report. Next, talk about ways to improve your draft.
2. **Make Changes** Think about your partner's suggestions. Use revision marks to make your changes.
   - Is the writing well-organized and smooth?

     > Earth is actually made up of layers. The crust is formed by large slabs of rock, called plates. The top layer is called the crust.

   - Make sure all the information is in your own words.

     > ~~Plate movement puts stress, or pressure, on the edges of a plate.~~
     > Sometimes the plates move and begin pushing against each other. This causes pressure along the edges of the plates.

Edit and Proofread

Work with a partner to edit and proofread your reports. Use revision marks to show your changes. Check all your facts.

Present

1. **On Your Own** Make a final copy of your research report. Add a list of sources at the end.
2. **With a Group** Work with your classmates to combine all the reports in a class book called "Forces of Nature." Or, you may want to turn your reports into a multimedia presentation.

Forces of Nature

Talk Together

In this unit, you found lots of answers to the **Big Question**. Now, use your concept map to discuss the **Big Question** with the class.

Concept Map

Write a Fact Sheet 

Choose on example from your concept map. Write a fact sheet about one of the forces that can change Earth's surface.

Share Your Ideas

Choose one of these ways to share your ideas about the **Big Question**.

Write It!

Make a Storyboard

Make a storyboard to show what causes a tsunami or how an island forms. Show the power of Earth in your drawings. Share your storyboard with the class.

Talk About It!

Give a News Report

Work with a partner. Pretend that a natural disaster, such as an earthquake or a tsunami, has taken place. You and your partner are the news team on the scene. Tell your classmates what is happening.

Do It!

Perform a Dance

Work with two or three classmates. Create a dance that represents a force of nature. What movements can you use to show a volcano erupting or a wave crashing down? Perform your dance for the class.

Write It!

Write an E-Mail

Pretend that you and your family members have just experienced a natural disaster. Write an e-mail telling a friend what happened.

Send Forward Delete

To: ann@eltngl.com/reachhigherseries;
From: kim@eltngl.com/reachhigherseries
Subject: Tsunami!
Attachment:

Hi, Ann,

Mom, Dad, and I are fine. We heard the tsunami warning siren and we left!

Unit 8

Getting There

BIG Question What tools can we use to achieve our goals?

RJUKAN, NORWAY
A boy making his way up during ice climbing

Unit at a Glance

- **Language Focus**: Ask for and Give Advice, Express Intentions
- **Reading Strategy**: Reading Strategy Review
- **Phonics Focus**: Suffixes: *-ant, -ent*; Words with More Than One Syllable
- **Topic**: Goals

Share What You Know

Do It!

1. **Draw** a picture of a treasure. Hide your picture in the classroom.
2. **Make** a treasure map. Show how to get to the treasure.
3. **Trade** maps with a partner. Find each other's treasure.

PART 1 **Language Focus**

Ask for and Give Advice

Listen to the dialogue between José and Marta. Then use **Language Frames** with a partner. Ask for and give advice about a goal you have.

Language Frames

- Do you know ______ ?
- Should I ______ ?
- You should/should not ______ .

Dialogue 

1.

2.

3.

Math Vocabulary

Key Words
distance
feet
kilometer
measurement
meter
unit

Key Words

Use Key Words and other words to talk about **units** of **measurement** in a race.

A 5K race

The race is called a 5K because runners cover a **distance** of five **kilometers**.

meter stick

- A **meter** is about 3 **feet**.
- A kilometer is 1,000 meters.

Talk Together

Suppose you want to train for a race. What tools could you use to achieve your goal? Use Language Frames from page 224 and Key Words to ask for and give advice with a partner.

Goal and Outcome

A **goal** is something you want to do or achieve. The **outcome** is what happens. Connecting a goal and the outcome helps you understand what you read, see, or hear.

Look at these pictures about José's goal. Read the text.

José wants to compete in a swim race.

He signs up for the race.

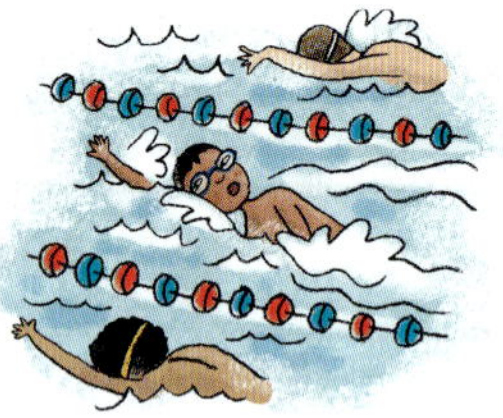

He trains a lot.

He competes in the big race.

Map and Talk

You can use a story map to show a goal and the outcome. To make one, write the goal in the square. Write the events in order in the circles. Put the outcome in the triangle.

Story Map

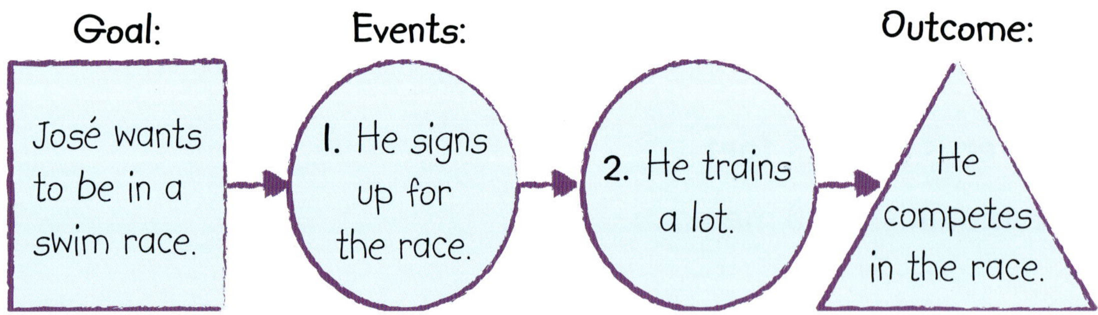

Tell a partner about a goal you wanted to achieve in your life and the outcome. Your partner makes a story map.

More Key Words

Use these words to talk about "Running Shoes" and "Two Clever Plans."

achieve

verb

To **achieve** means to get something that you work for. She worked hard to **achieve** first place.

direction

noun

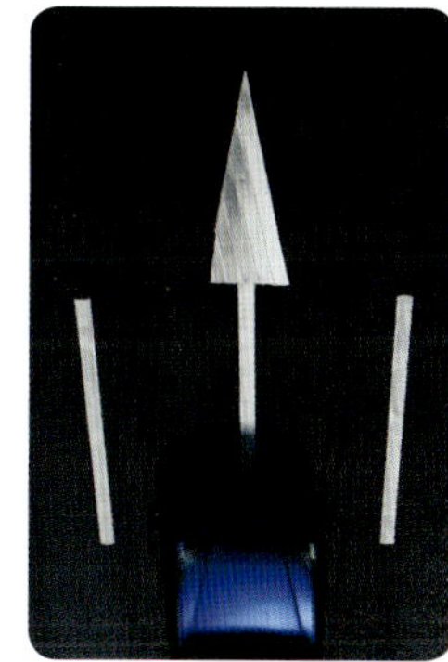

When you move toward something, you move in that **direction**. The arrow shows the **direction** of the road.

estimate

verb

When you make a guess about something, you **estimate**. Can you **estimate** how many coins are in the jar?

goal

noun

A **goal** is something that you want to do. His **goal** is to catch the ball.

strategy

noun

A **strategy** is a plan for success. She has a **strategy** for winning.

Talk Together

Make a Vocabulary Example Chart for each **Key Word**. Then compare your charts with a partner's.

Word	Definition	My Example
strategy	a plan	my soccer team's plan to win

PART 1 **Reading Strategy**

Choose Reading Strategies

Good readers know that they need different **strategies** to understand different texts. Often, you use more than one strategy. It is important to know which strategies to use and when to use them. As you read:

- Think about the different strategies. Each one is a tool that can help you understand the text.
- Know what you are reading. Some strategies work better than others for different kinds of texts.
- Switch or add strategies if you need to. The more you read, the easier it gets to change strategies. Even the best readers switch and add!

When you read, choose a reading strategy to help you understand.

Reading Strategies

- Plan and Monitor
- Ask Questions
- Make Inferences
- Determine Importance
- Make Connections
- Visualize
- Synthesize

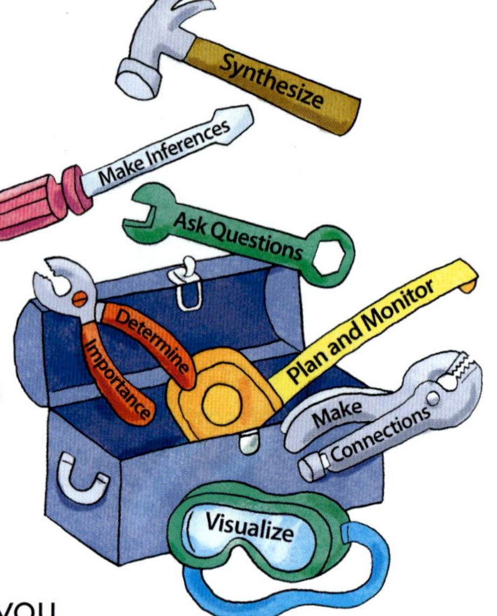

How to Choose a Reading Strategy

1. Think about what you are trying to understand.

2. Decide which strategy you can use to help you understand.

3. Think about how the strategy helped you.

I want to know _____.

I can _____.

That strategy helped me _____.

Talk Together

Read José's letter. Tell a partner which reading strategies you used to help you understand the text.

Letter

May 27, 20____

Dear Manuela,

It was great to see you at the Junior Olympics. I'm sorry I was unable to talk to you before you left. But I'm glad you were there to cheer me on. I couldn't hear your shouts while I was in the water. I could barely tell if I was swimming in the right **direction**! But, your support really meant a lot. Thank you!

I plan to reenter the Junior Olympics next year. My **goal** is to win the 400-**meter** race. Four hundred meters is about a quarter mile. That's a long **distance** to swim at top speed. My trainer **estimates** I'll need to train six days a week to **achieve** the strength I'll need. That's a lot of work!

Mom tells me you plan to rejoin the city swim team. I was unaware that you had dropped out! Mom also told me that you spent the summer in Miami. I'll bet you had some great swims on those sunny beaches!

I'll see you at this year's family reunion. I can hardly wait. Maybe then you could teach me a good **strategy** for long-distance swimming. I'm going to need all the help I can get!

Your cousin,

José

PART 1 **Phonics Focus**

Suffixes: -ant, -ent

attendant

present

Listen and Learn

Listen to the ending syllables of the words in the box. Then sort the words by how that syllable is spelled.

distant	servant	president	different
pleasant	accident	immigrant	student

-ant

______
______
______
______

-ent

______
______
______
______

Complete each sentence with a word from the lists above.

1. The ______ star did not give much light.

2. My family had a ______ afternoon at the park.

3. I am a ______ at my school.

4. I chose a ______ color because I don't like red.

Talk Together

Listen and read. Find the words that end with the suffixes *-ant* and *-ent.*

Over to You

The Mountain

It was Amir's goal to climb the distant mountain. His big brother and his dad had already made it to the top. Amir was different. He had not climbed the mountain yet. Amir read about the mountain. He read the distance from the bottom to the top. He didn't think the climb would be pleasant.

"It's 14,000 feet (4,267 meters) high," he told his dad.

"It's not easy, but I'm confident you can do this. First, you need a training strategy," his dad said. "You can be my student. It is important for you to get ready first."

"Should I lift weights and climb stairs?"

"Yes, you should. And I'll join you for a run every day."

"Do you know how long the training will take?" asked Amir.

"I estimate it will take two or three months," his dad said.

So, Amir began his training. Soon, he felt more confident about the climb.

One morning, three months later, the moment came. It was time for Amir to achieve his goal. He was ready to climb that mountain.

Work with a partner.

Find and list the words with the suffixes *-ant* and *-ent*. Sort the words according to their suffixes.

Practice reading words with the suffixes *-ant* and *-ent* by reading "The Mountain" with a partner.

Read a Story

Genre

Realistic fiction is a made-up story that sounds like real life. This story is circular. It ends the same way it began.

Character's Motive

A **motive** is the reason a character does something.

> Once a year, a man came from the city in a red jeep. The village people called him the number man. **He counted the number of people in the village for the government.**

This character comes to the village because he wants to do his job. That's his motive.

Running Shoes

by Frederick Lipp

illustrated by Jason Gaillard

Set a Purpose
Find out why Sophy wants a pair of running shoes.

Sophy lived in a land where it was nearly always hot and sunny. When it finally rained, it rained for days and nights without end.

One terribly hot day, Sophy squinted her eyes against the blinding sun. The air was still. Suddenly, a noise like bees **swarming** from a tree grew louder and louder. The pig began **snorting**. The chickens **cackled**.

Sophy sat up straight like a **bamboo shoot**. "Must be the number man's jeep," she thought as she rubbed her eyes.

swarming flying in a group
snorting breathing loudly
cackled made loud noises
bamboo shoot tall plant

Once a year, a man came from the city in a red jeep. The village people called him the number man. He counted the number of people in the village for the government.

After **making the rounds**, the number man stopped at Sophy's house. "How many people live here?" he asked.

"Two," Sophy answered. "My mother and I."

"Let's see, that comes to one hundred fifty-four people in the village. Last year there were . . ." The number man stopped. He had heard that Sophy's father had died because there was no doctor or hospital near the village.

making the rounds counting all the other people

Sophy stared at the man's shoes.

"Ah, you have never seen running shoes before?" the man asked.

Sophy blushed. She thought about **her secret wish**. Her wish felt far, far away like a **hawk lazily soaring** in circles in the sky. Deep in her heart she knew her wish would come true if she had a pair of shoes like the number man's.

"Walk with me to the river," the number man said.

Sophy blushed Sophy's face turned red from embarrassment

her secret wish something she really wanted that no one else knew about

hawk lazily soaring bird flying slowly

"Stick your feet into the clay. Now step out." Sophy liked the warm feeling of mud **squishing** between her toes.

The number man took a stick with lots of numbers from his pocket. He **measured** Sophy's footprints.

Then the number man rubbed his chin as he **mumbled** numbers to himself. "Let's see. . . . In about a month, you will receive a surprise."

squishing moving
measured checked the length of
mumbled said in a low voice

Sophy counted the days until a **postal van** drove through the village and dropped off a **package** by her door. She held her breath as she tore open the package.

"Running shoes!" she yelled. She carefully put on each shoe. "Now my wish will come true."

"What wish?" her mother asked.

"I want to go to school."

"But the school is eight **kilometers** away over horrible roads."

"Yes, but now I have running shoes!" Sophy said as she bounced up and down.

postal van mail truck
package box

A smile slowly came over her mother's face. She remembered how Sophy's father used to sit with Sophy in the shade of a coconut tree and write marks on a small blackboard. He called them *words*. "This word is your name, Sophy, and this is the name of our village," he explained.

"You may go to school," Sophy's mother said.

Before You Continue

1. **Character's Motive** Why does Sophy want her own pair of running shoes? How are they part of her secret wish?
2. **Make Inferences** What do you know about Sophy's father? How would you describe him?

Predict

What will happen when Sophy goes to school?

The next day before the sun rose, Sophy ate a bowl of rice and a little salt fish. Then she **set off** through the rice fields, running.

The shoes protected her feet from the sharp, red rocks. She **sailed through the air** like a skipping stone over water.

Jumping over little streams, Sophy ran through the **jungle** on a **narrow, winding** road. She ran faster and faster until finally she saw the one-room schoolhouse.

set off began her journey
sailed through the air moved quickly
jungle plants and trees
narrow, winding thin, twisting

Children's **sandals** were lined up outside the door.

Sophy **hurriedly** untied her running shoes, placed them by the door, and walked barefoot into the schoolroom.

"My name is Sophy. I want to learn how to read and write."

The class, all boys, **giggled**.

"Quiet," the teacher said. "Come, you are welcome here. Where did you come from?"

"Andong Kralong."

The teacher **gasped**. "That is eight **kilometers** away!"

"Yes, Miss, but I have running shoes!"

sandals open shoes worn in warm weather ▶
hurriedly quickly
giggled laughed quietly
gasped was surprised

The boys covered their teeth as they laughed. Tears rose in Sophy's eyes. "I want to learn how to read."

"But you're a girl," one boy whispered.

Sophy **pulled all her courage together** like a green snake ready to **strike**. She waited for the right time to speak.

After school, Sophy tied on her running shoes with three knots in each shoe. She looked over at the boys and said, "If you think you are so smart, try to catch me."

pulled all her courage together became brave enough to do something

strike bite

The boys pushed and shoved each other out of the way. They ran after Sophy. No one could catch her.

The next morning, Sophy woke **before the rooster's first call**. **Her head start** allowed her to arrive at school before there were any sandals lined up at the door. When the boys **paraded** into the classroom, they smiled shyly.

They remembered how Sophy had won the race.

From that day on, Sophy learned many subjects taught at the one-room schoolhouse.

before the rooster's first call very early
Her head start Leaving early
paraded came

▸ Before You Continue

1. **Confirm Prediction** Use your own words to tell what happens on Sophy's first day at school. Was your prediction right?
2. **Character's Motive** Why does Sophy challenge the boys to a race?

Predict
The number man comes to the village again. What will Sophy do?

One morning a year later, Sophy was sitting with her mother when they saw a cloud of dust suddenly rise over the hill.

The pig began snorting. The chickens cackled.

It was the number man coming in his red jeep.

In that moment, the first **sprinkle** of rain made little circles in the river. The circles grew larger. **Monsoon** was beginning.

Sophy looked up at the gathering clouds and thought she would be cooler in her daily race to school.

sprinkle small drops
Monsoon The rainy season

The number man counted everyone in the village.

At the end of the day, he arrived at Sophy's house.

The number man looked down at Sophy's bare feet.

"Where are your running shoes?" he asked.

Sophy smiled and put her hands on her hips. "I only wear my running shoes when I go to school," she said.

They both laughed.

"I have something for you this time," Sophy said. "Follow me."

They walked to the side of the river. Sophy held a bamboo stick and scratched words into the clay:

Thank you for the running shoes.
Now I can read and write.

Everything was so quiet that Sophy could hear the stream **bubbling** around the stones. She looked down and said shyly, "One day I want to help my people build a school and . . . "

"What?" the number man asked.

"I want to be the teacher," Sophy said, smiling and **wiggling her toes** in the mud. ❖

bubbling making soft sounds
wiggling her toes quickly moving her toes up and down

▸ Before You Continue

1. **Confirm Prediction** Was your prediction correct? What does Sophy do when the number man returns?
2. **Genre** Why do you think "Running Shoes" is a circular story?

Meet the Author

AWARD WINNER

Frederick Lipp

Sophy is a fictional character, but her story is real for many Cambodian girls. Frederick Lipp wrote "Running Shoes" to show how difficult it is for girls like Sophy to get an education.

To help educate girls in rural Cambodia, Mr. Lipp created an organization called the Cambodian Arts and Scholarship Foundation. The program gives girls in poor villages the money and support they need to go to school. Mr. Lipp visits Cambodia twice a year to check his organization's progress and visit with students.

◀ Frederick Lipp

Writing Tip

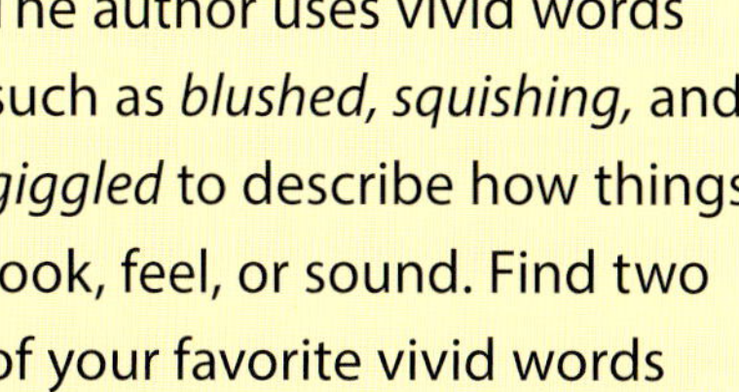

The author uses vivid words such as *blushed, squishing,* and *giggled* to describe how things look, feel, or sound. Find two of your favorite vivid words from the story. Then write a sentence using the words.

PART 1 **Think and Respond**

Key Words	
achieve	kilometer
direction	measurement
distance	meter
estimate	strategy
feet	unit
goal	

Talk About It

1. How do you know that the story is **realistic fiction**?

   I know that the story is realistic fiction because _____.

2. Suppose Sophy **asks for advice** on her first day of school. The teacher **gives her advice**. What might they each say?

   Sophy: How _____? What should I _____?
   Teacher: You should/should not _____.

3. When Sophy goes to school, how do the boys treat her? What makes them change?

   The boys _____. They change when _____.

Write About It

Imagine you are Sophy. Write a journal entry to your father. Explain how the running shoes helped you **achieve** your **goal** of going to school. Use **Key Words**.

Hi, Dad,
My running shoes _____.

Reread and Summarize

Goal and Outcome

Make a story map for "Running Shoes."

Story Map

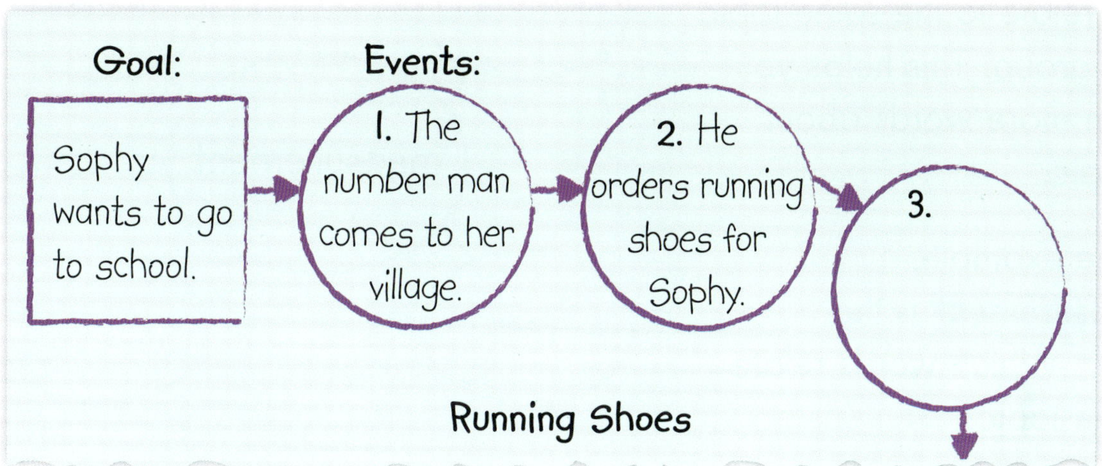

Use your story map to summarize the story for a partner. Use the sentence frames and **Key Words**. Then explain how the events influence a future event, or the outcome. Record your discussion.

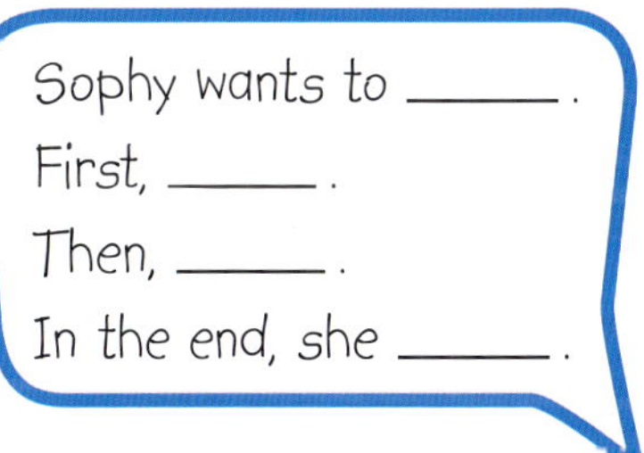

Fluency

Practice reading with intonation. Rate your reading.

Talk Together

Find pictures in the story that show how the number man helps Sophy **achieve** her **goal**. Explain the pictures to a partner. Use **Key Words**.

PART 1 **Word Work**

Word Categories

When you make a **word category**, you put words that relate to the same topic in a group. This helps you learn more words about a topic.

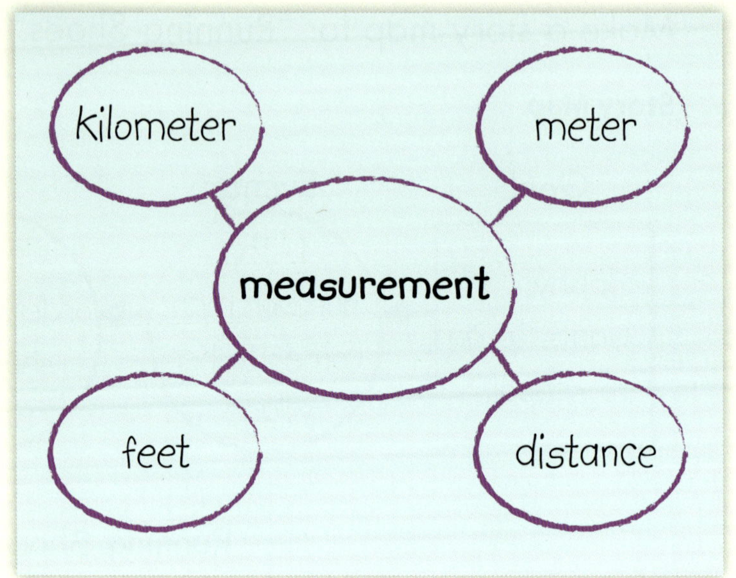

In the example, **measurement** is the topic. Which words relate to the topic?

Try It Together

Read the passage. Then complete each item.

My brother's goal is to learn how to cook. His strategy is to cook two meals a week for our family. I think he will achieve his goal, but I am not looking forward to those meals!

1. **Goal and strategy could be placed in a category of words about _____ .**
   - **A** time
   - **B** meals
   - **C** success
   - **D** measurement

2. **Which word is in the same category as goal and strategy?**
   - **A** cook
   - **B** week
   - **C** family
   - **D** achieve

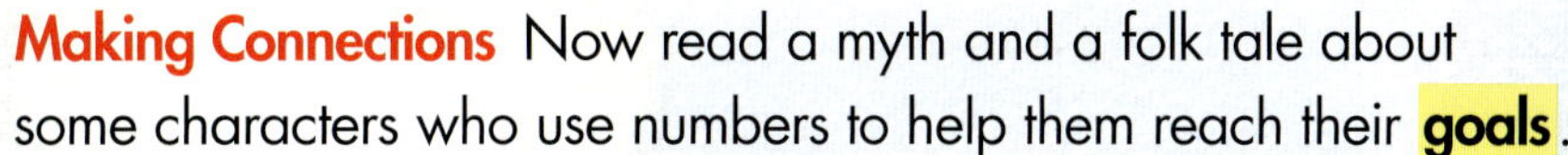

Making Connections Now read a myth and a folk tale about some characters who use numbers to help them reach their **goals**.

Genre A **myth** is a very old story that often has gods and goddesses as characters. A **folk tale** is a story that people have told over and over. It often has animals as characters.

TWO CLEVER PLANS

In these stories, find out what two **clever** characters do to reach their **goals**.

clever smart

Before You Continue

1. **Preview and Predict** Read the title and the text. Look at the picture. What do you think the stories will be about?
2. **Genre** Do you think the story about the turtle will be realistic? Explain.

THREE GOLDEN APPLES

a Greek myth retold by **Colleen Pellier**
Illustrated by **Raúl Colón**

Atalanta lived long ago in Greece. Her father, King Iasius, wanted her to marry, but Atalanta had her own ideas. "I'll only marry the man who can beat me in a race!" she said.

Of course, the beautiful young woman didn't **intend** to become any man's wife. She was the fastest runner in the land. No man would **outrun** *her.*

Day after day, **eager young men** tried, but each one failed. "I'll be free forever," Atalanta thought.

intend plan
outrun run faster than
eager young men young men who wanted to win

Melanion, one of **her suitors**, watched the races with sadness. He was in love with Atalanta, but how could he **outrun** her?

He begged Aphrodite, the goddess of love, for help. The kind goddess led him into her garden. Flowers bloomed on every bush. Their sweet **perfume** made Melanion think of Atalanta even more. Aphrodite **paused** under a tree in the center of the garden. She plucked three golden apples and handed them to the young man. "No one can **resist** these," she said.

her suitors the men who wanted to marry Atalanta
perfume smell
paused stopped
resist say no to

Before You Continue

1. **Clarify** If Atalanta does not want to marry, why does she offer to marry any man who can outrun her? Explain her thinking.
2. **Character's Motive** Why does Melanion want to win the race?

Melanion chose the next day to race Atalanta. The two runners stood side by side, waiting to begin. Atalanta's golden hair streamed down her back. Her eyes sparkled like the jewels in her father's crown. **At the signal**, she shot ahead like an arrow.

Melanion rolled the first apple off the path and Atalanta **darted** after it. She scooped it up and flew past him again.

Melanion tossed the second apple farther. Atalanta **swerved** off the course to **grasp** it. Soon she was beside him again. She sailed ahead, her hair blowing behind her.

At the signal As soon as the race started

darted ran

swerved turned

grasp grab

Melanion **flung** the last apple as far as he could. It glittered in the grass, and Atalanta dashed after it. It took her only seconds to reach him again. Melanion's muscles burned with pain, but he pushed harder. With a final burst of energy, he shot over the finish line.

"That's unfair!" Atalanta cried. "I had to run three times as far to get these apples!"

But **a smile touched her lips**. Melanion was not as fast as she was, but he would make a handsome, clever husband. ❖

flung threw
a smile touched her lips she smiled

Before You Continue

1. **Visualize** What words help you picture Atalanta in your mind?
2. **Goal/Outcome** Explain the **strategy** Melanion used to reach his **goal**.

TURTLE AND HIS FOUR COUSINS

a Cuban folk tale retold by **Margaret Read MacDonald**
Illustrated by **Raúl Colón**

"Hey, Slow Poke Turtle! Move those little legs!" called Deer. Deer made fun of other creatures. Turtle didn't care.

"Slow Poke yourself! I am faster than you," he **muttered**.

"Ha!" snorted Deer. "Look at my long legs! Want to RACE?"

Turtle stopped. "Hmm, I wonder . . ." he mumbled. Then he had an idea. "Meet me tomorrow at the beach. We will race all the way to the fourth hill."

Deer ran off laughing. "Tomorrow you LOSE!" he called.

muttered said quietly

Turtle went to see his four cousins. "Cousin Number One, I want you to go to the first hill. Cousin Number Two, go to the second hill. You, Third Cousin, go to the third hill. Cousin Number Four, I want you to meet Deer at the beach to start the race."

Then Turtle slowly made his way to the fourth hill and waited.

Deer arrived on the beach, singing his proud song. "Deer Long Legs! Fast! Fast! Fast! Deer Long Legs! Fast! Fast! Fast!"

Cousin Number Four sang, too. "Turtle is here. Here. Here. Here."

▸ Before You Continue

1. **Character's Motive** Why does Deer challenge Turtle to a race?
2. **Ask Questions** Do you have any questions about Turtle's plan? What are they? How can you find the answers?

The race began. Deer ran off SO fast. The turtle moved slowly through the sand.

Deer reached the first hill! He sang his song to **prove** he was there. “Deer Long Legs! Fast! Fast! Fast!”

Then he heard a little voice in the grass. “Turtle is here. Here. Here. Here.”

“What?” Deer cried. He ran faster to the second hill. “Deer Long Legs! Fast! Fast! Fast!”

But a tiny voice answered, “Turtle is here. Here. Here. Here.”

“Not POSSIBLE!” thought Deer. He ran faster.

prove show

Deer reached the third hill. He was out of breath. "Deer Long Legs . . . Fast, fast, fast . . ."

Then he heard, "Turtle is here! Here. Here. Here."

"NO!" Deer cried, **stumbling along** to the last hill. He could hardly breathe. "Fourth hill! I win," he **gasped**. "Deer Long Legs . . ."

But someone was already singing. "Turtle is here. Here! Here! Here!" Then Turtle said in a **mocking** voice, "Sorry, Long Legs. Short Legs won the race."

After that, if Deer felt like making fun of somebody, he just **kept his comments to himself**. ❖

stumbling along running and falling
gasped said out of breath
mocking teasing
kept his comments to himself did not say anything

Before You Continue

1. **Clarify** What happens to Deer on each hill?
2. **Goal/Outcome** What is Turtle's goal? Does he get what he wants? Explain.

PART 1 Respond and Extend

Compare Settings

Key Words

achieve	kilometer
direction	measurement
distance	meter
estimate	strategy
feet	unit
goal	

"Three Golden Apples" and "Turtle and His Four Cousins" have different settings. Where does each story take place? When does each story happen? Complete the comparison chart with a partner.

Comparison Chart

	"Three Golden Apples"	"Turtle and His Four Cousins"
Where	Greece	
When		

Look back at the pictures in the stories with your partner. Use the pictures and your chart to compare and contrast the settings.

Talk Together

Now think about Melanion in the myth and Turtle in the folk tale. What tools help them **achieve** their **goals**? Use **Key Words** in your discussion.

Past Tense

Regular past-tense verbs end in *-ed*, but **irregular** past-tense verbs do not.

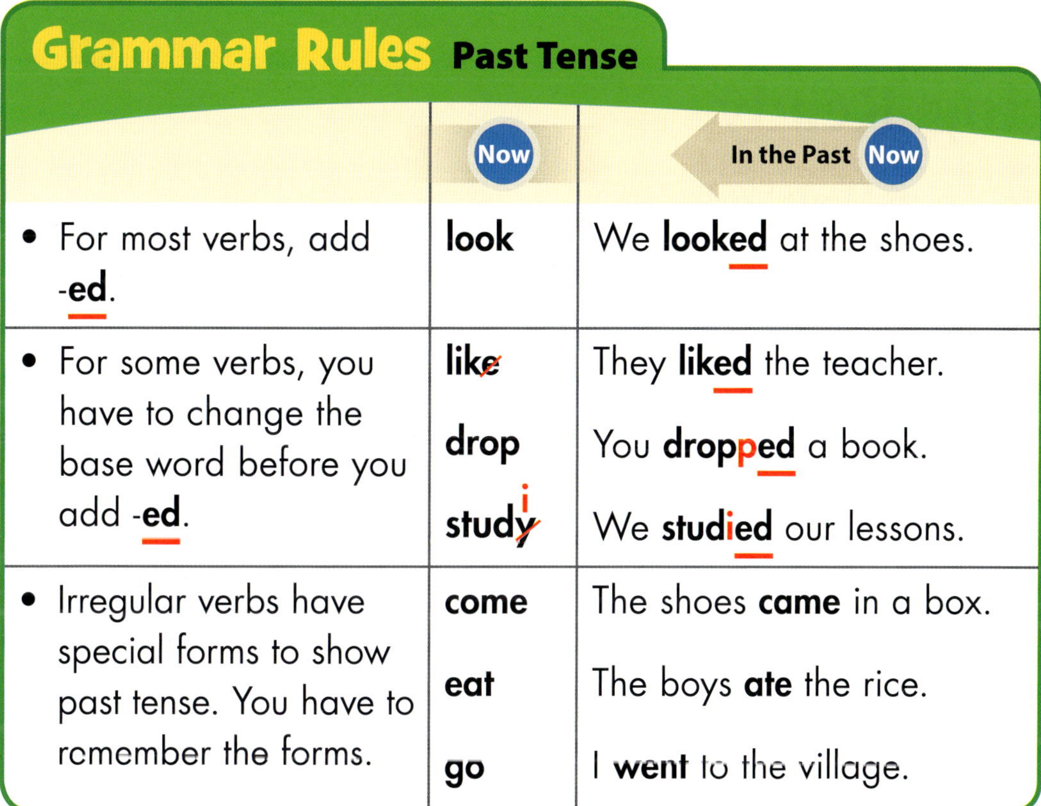

Grammar Rules Past Tense

	Now	In the Past / Now
• For most verbs, add -**ed**.	**look**	We **looked** at the shoes.
• For some verbs, you have to change the base word before you add -**ed**.	**like** **drop** **study**	They **liked** the teacher. You **dropped** a book. We **studied** our lessons.
• Irregular verbs have special forms to show past tense. You have to remember the forms.	**come** **eat** **go**	The shoes **came** in a box. The boys **ate** the rice. I **went** to the village.

Read Past-Tense Verbs

Read this passage from "Running Shoes." Identify one regular past-tense verb and one irregular past-tense verb.

> Once a year, a man came from the city in a red jeep. The village people called him the number man.

Write Past-Tense Verbs 

What happened on page 241? Write three sentences and read them to a partner. Use regular and irregular past-tense verbs.

PART 2 Language Focus

Express Intentions

Listen to Emma's song. Then use **Language Frames** to express intentions about a goal you have.

Getting Ready

I want to go to New York City.
I will pack my walking shoes.
I plan to see so many places
On the streets and avenues.

I will visit the museums.
I am going to see the zoo.
I'll take pictures to remember
All the things I see and do.

Tune: "Clementine"

Language Frames

- I want to ______.
- I will ______.
- I plan to ______.
- I am going to ______.

Song

Social Studies Vocabulary

Key Words
continent
destination
globe
journey
location

Key Words

Use **Key Words** and other words to talk about an exciting **journey**.

- Look at different **locations** on a **globe**.
- Which one would you like to visit? Which **continent** is it on?
- Point to your **destination**.

globe

Talk Together

Pretend that you plan to go on a journey. Use **Language Frames** from page 262 and **Key Words** to express your intentions to a partner. Then tell how you will achieve your goal.

Main Idea and Details

When you talk about something, you start with the **main idea**. Then you give **details** about the main idea. Connecting the main idea and details helps you understand what you read, see, or hear.

Look at these pictures. They show how Emma and her aunt plan for a trip to New York City. Read the text.

They save money.

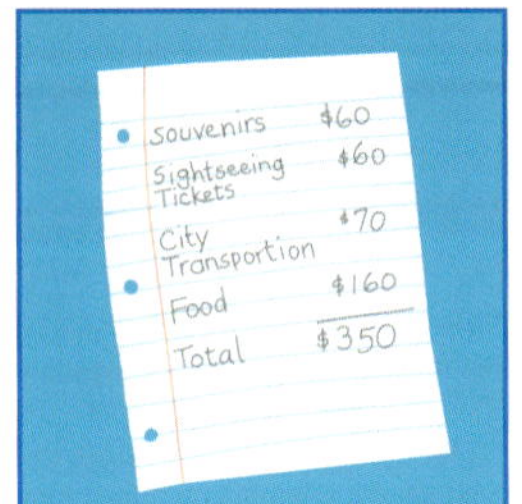

They make a budget.

They pick places to see.

Map and Talk

You can use a main idea diagram to show the most important idea and details that support it. To make one, write the main idea on the line on the left side. Write the details on the lines on the right side.

Main Idea Diagram

Main Idea	Details
Emma and her aunt plan for a trip.	They save money.
	They make a budget.
	They pick places to see.

Talk Together

Make a main idea diagram with this main idea: **There are many interesting places to visit**. Share your diagram with a partner.

Academic Vocabulary

More Key Words

Use these words to talk about "One Man's Goal" and "Climbing Toward Her Goal."

challenge
noun

A **challenge** is something that is hard to do. It is a **challenge** to climb up a rope.

discover
verb

When you **discover** something, you find it. She **discovers** an insect on this plant.

endurance
noun

When you have **endurance**, you keep doing something. A long race takes **endurance**.

explore
verb

To **explore** means to go somewhere to learn about people or things. He **explores** a new area.

prepare
verb

To **prepare** means to get ready for something. She packs a suitcase to **prepare** for her trip.

Talk Together

Ask a question using a **Key Word**. A partner answers with a different **Key Word**.

Why do you want to explore the ocean?

I would like to discover new kinds of fish.

PART 2 **Reading Strategy**

- Plan and Monitor
- Ask Questions
- Make Inferences
- Determine Importance
- Make Connections
- Visualize
- Synthesize

Use Reading Strategies

When do you use reading strategies? Good readers use strategies all the time! Get in the habit of using reading strategies before, during, and after you read. Here's how to read actively:

- Look through the text quickly. What is the text mostly about? Decide on your purpose, or reason, for reading.

- As you read, stop now and then to ask yourself, "Does this make sense?" Use a reading strategy to help you understand better.

- When you finish reading, stop and think. Decide what you gained from reading the text.

How to Use a Reading Strategy

1. Before you start to read a text, ask yourself, "What strategies can help me get ready to read?"

2. During reading, think about what strategies can help you understand.

3. After reading, ask yourself, "What strategies can I use to help me think about what I read?"

Before I read, I will _____.

As I read, I can _____.

Now that I'm done, I think _____.

Talk Together

Read Emma's diary entries about her trip to New York City. Tell a partner which reading strategies you used to help you understand the text.

Diary

Thursday, July 15

Today we saw animals. First we **explored** the Children's Zoo on 64th Street. What an adventure! At the petting zoo, I touched the tame horses and a sheep. A woolly alpaca nibbled corn right out of my hand. It tickled!

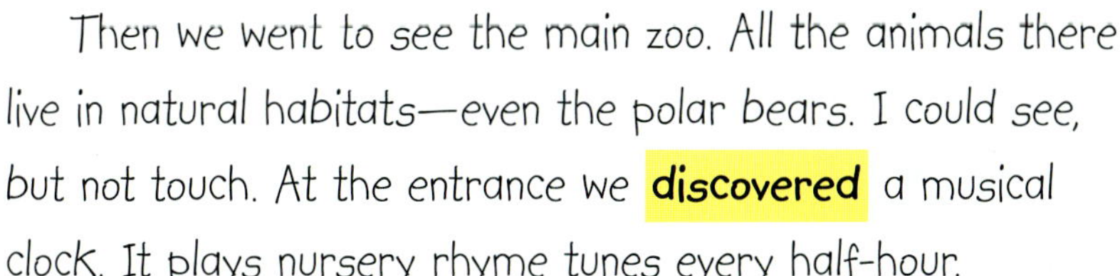

Then we went to see the main zoo. All the animals there live in natural habitats—even the polar bears. I could see, but not touch. At the entrance we **discovered** a musical clock. It plays nursery rhyme tunes every half-hour.

Friday, July 16

Today we go home. This morning we took the ferry to see one last sight: the Statue of Liberty. I climbed all 354 steps up to Lady Liberty's crown. That really tested my **endurance**, but the view from the top was worth it.

To **prepare** for the long **journey** home, we stopped at a shop in the train station. Aunt Rita bought some magazines. I bought a book. Luckily, I had enough money. Trying to stay within the budget has been a real **challenge**, but I still have $12.35 left over!

PART 2 **Phonics Focus**

Words with More Than One Syllable

pa/per
2 vowel sounds = 2 syllables

re/cy/cle
3 vowel sounds = 3 syllables

al/li/ga/tor
4 vowel sounds = 4 syllables

Listen and Learn

Listen to each word. Count the vowel sounds you hear. Decide how many syllables each word has.

1. respect ______
2. rabbit ______
3. decoration ______
4. unfriendly ______
5. delicious ______
6. magnificent ______

Talk Together

Listen and read. Use what you know about syllables, prefixes, and suffixes to read longer words.

Over to You

Explore the Unknown

One day, I want to travel the globe. I want to see things I have not seen before. People have always explored the unknown. They wanted a challenge. These people crossed continents. Their journeys took them to unexplored locations. Marco Polo was the first explorer to travel over land to Asia. The trip took him years. Christopher Columbus tried to find Asia, too. He took a sea route. He didn't find Asia. But he did find America. Other explorers went to the Arctic. Many of these trips were unsuccessful. Many were successful.

It will not take me years to get somewhere. I will not be going to unexplored destinations. But these countries will be new for me. I plan to explore them. I want to see new things. I want to meet new people.

There is one place left to explore. Who knows where it is? Outer space! I might decide to explore outer space. That would be exciting!

Work with a partner.

Find words with more than one syllable in the passage. Make a list and decide how many syllables each word has.

Practice reading words with more than one syllable by reading "Explore the Unknown" with a partner.

Read a Human Interest Feature

Genre

A **human interest feature** tells about a person's interesting experiences or adventures.

Text Features

A **map** is a drawing that gives information about places. A **compass rose** shows the directions north, south, east, and west. A **legend** explains the pictures or symbols on a map.

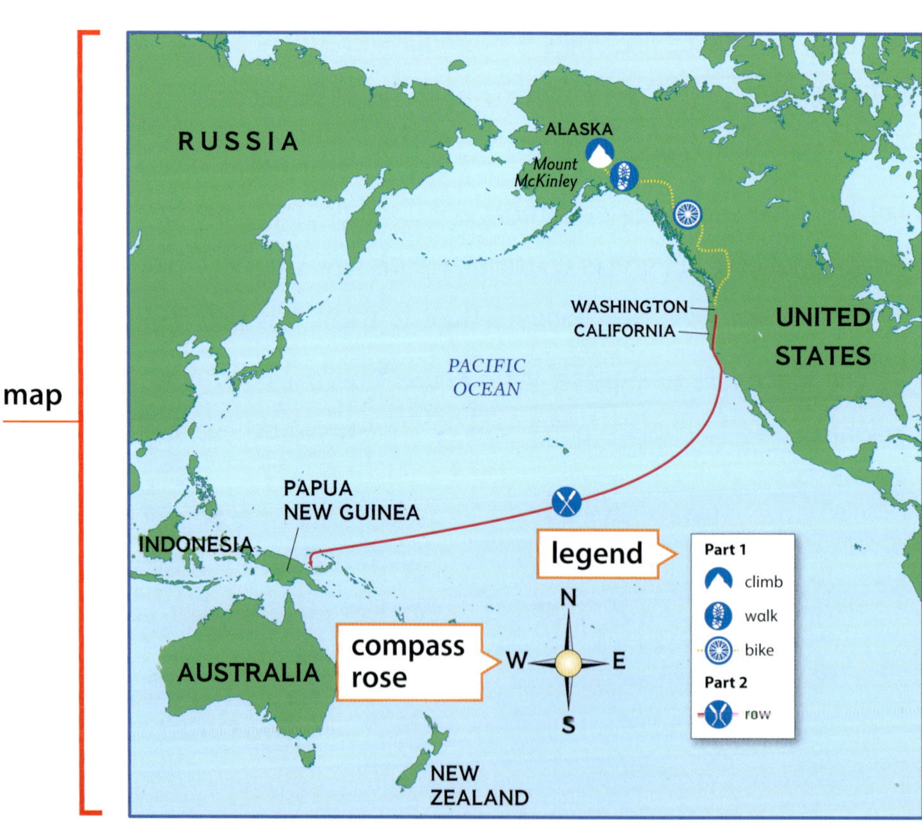

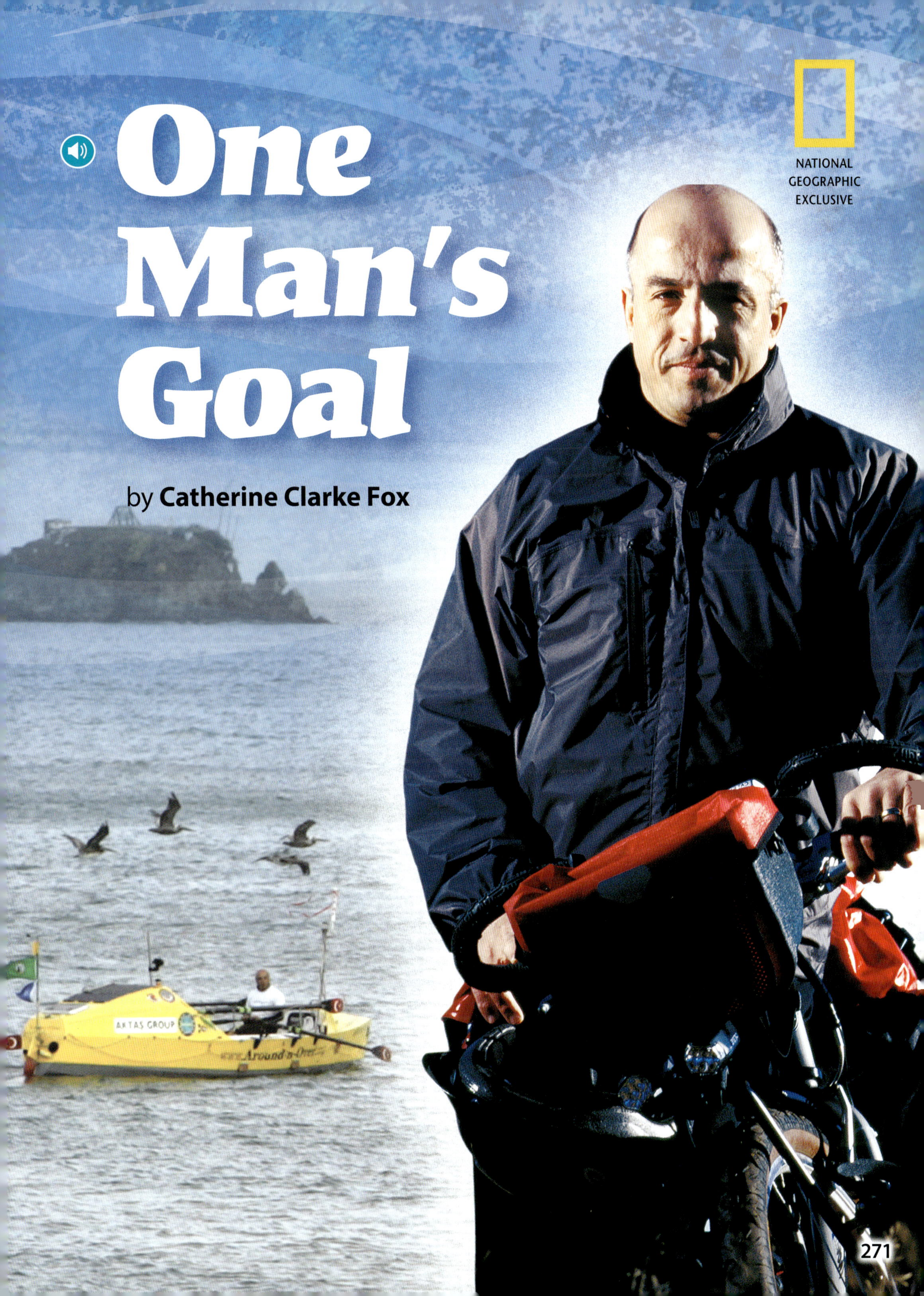

One Man's Goal

by **Catherine Clarke Fox**

Set a Purpose
Learn about the **challenges** a man faced during his amazing **journey**.

Around the World

Erden Eruç left California on July 10, 2007 in his 23-foot-long boat. He was rowing across the Pacific Ocean toward Australia. Birds, fish, and sharks were his only **company**.

Eruç rowed his boat across the Pacific Ocean toward Australia.

company visitors

Crossing the Pacific was amazing, but that was only part of Eruç's **journey**. He was determined to go around the world—using his own **energy**!

During his journey, Eruç wanted to climb the tallest **peaks** on six **continents** to **honor the memory of** a fellow climber. Eruç planned to bike, walk, climb, and row the world—without any motors to help him.

bike

row

climb

energy power
peaks mountain tops
honor the memory of help others remember

Before You Continue

1. **Classify** How did Eruç plan to travel around the world? Name the different ways.
2. **Make Inferences** What kind of person is Eruç? What makes you think so?

A Two-Part Adventure

For the first **leg** of his trip, Eruç bicycled 5,546 miles from Seattle, Washington, to Mount McKinley in Alaska and back. When he was in Alaska, he walked 67 miles to **base camp**. Then he climbed McKinley's peak, which is 20,320 feet high.

For the second part of his adventure, Eruç rowed toward Australia.

▲ **Eruç tells kids about his journey to inspire them to dream and try to reach their own goals.**

leg part

base camp the camp at the bottom of the mountain where supplies are kept

Erden Eruç's Adventure

▶ Before You Continue

1. **Sequence** According to the text, what did Eruç do after he bicycled to Alaska but before he left for Australia?
2. **Use Text Features** Look at the map legend. What does the most southern symbol on the map and the place name shown in blue tell you about Eruç's **journey**?

Alone on the Ocean

Traveling alone wasn't easy. Eruç **faced some disappointments** and **challenges**.

For example, he had to row at least 10 hours a day, so he brought along a music player. He hoped to listen to music and books and study Spanish to pass the time. Unfortunately, there was a lot of **tropical rain**. So Eruç had to pack his player away to keep it safe and dry.

Eruç rowed alone for many hours a day.

faced some disappointments had difficult times

tropical rain rain from hot, wet areas

On the Way to Australia

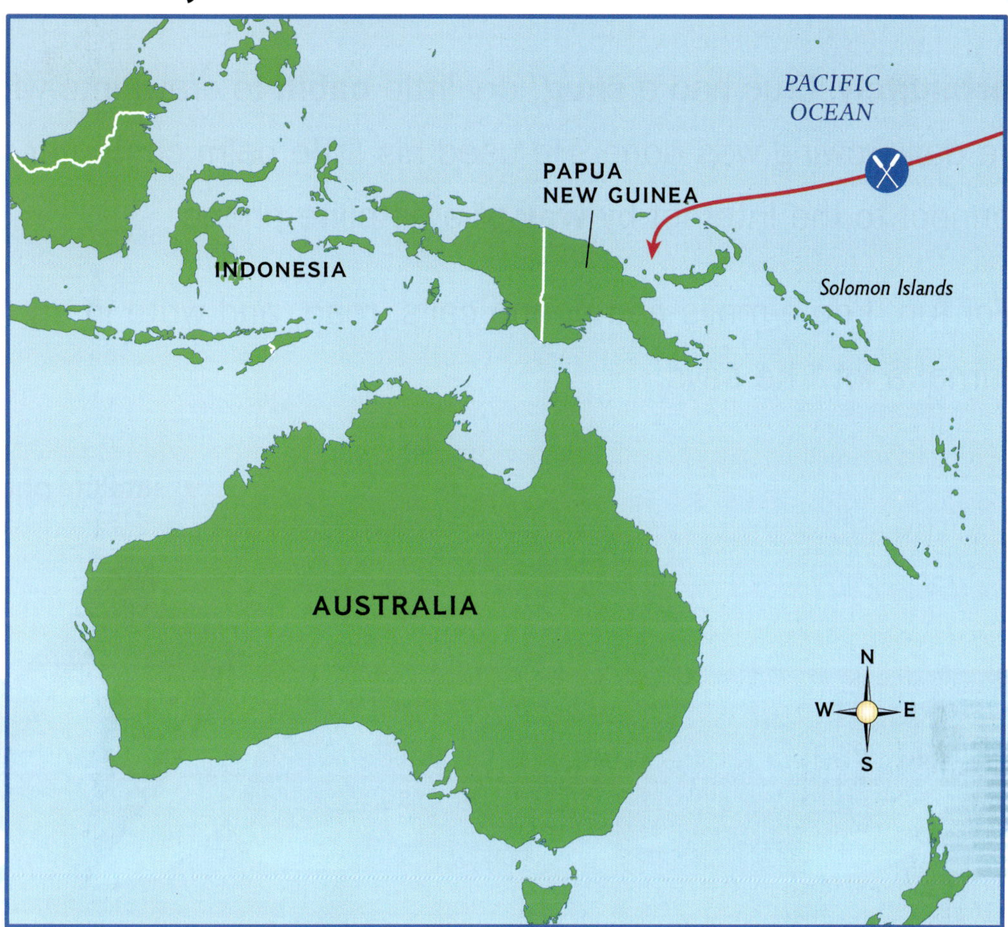

Not only that, but wind and waves kept pushing him **westward**. He wanted to go south toward the Solomon Islands. Big ships have powerful engines, but Eruç's rowboat and arm-power were **no match for** the winds.

If his luck didn't change, he would have to change his plan. He would try to land at Papua New Guinea. And, that's what happened! Eruç finally reached Papua New Guinea in February 2009.

westward to the west
no match for not as strong as

Before You Continue

1. **Visualize** What do you hear, feel, and see in your mind as you read about Eruç's **journey**?
2. **Use Text Features** Use the compass rose. What is south of Papua New Guinea?

A Home on the Waves

Fortunately, Eruç had a **snug**, dry little **cabin** to crawl into when the daily rowing was done. He used his little palm computer to connect to the Internet **by way of** a satellite phone.

"For fun, I do e-mails and phone calls, read, and write in my journal a lot," he says.

▼ satellite phone

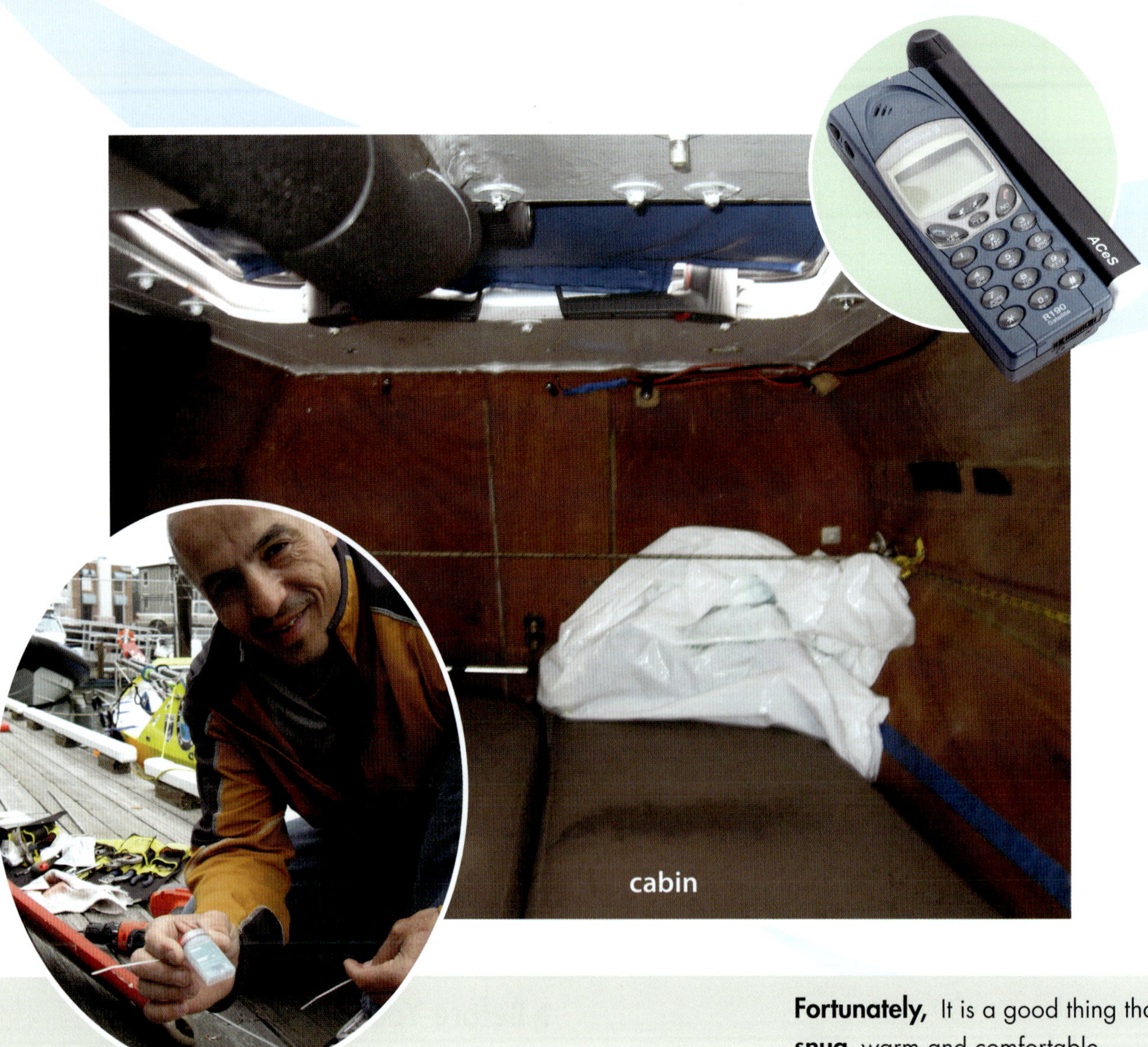

cabin

▲ Eruç measures the water temperature with a special tool.

Fortunately, It is a good thing that
snug warm and comfortable
cabin room
by way of using

Protein bars gave him energy. He boiled water on a one-burner stove to **prepare** **freeze-dried** meals.

Using **solar panels**, he charged the batteries on his boat. Then he used an electric-powered machine to remove salt from the ocean water so he could drink it. But this only worked when the sun was shining. Because of the tropical rains, he often had to use a different machine with a handle he could pump by hand to remove salt from the water.

▲ **Eruç used a machine to make salty ocean water safe to drink.**

one-burner stove ▶

Protein bars Healthy snacks
freeze-dried easy-to-make
solar panels objects that collect heat from the sun and turn it into energy

▶ Before You Continue

1. **Classify** Eruç has many pieces of equipment on his boat. What are they?
2. **Clarify** Why did Eruç need a different machine to remove salt from water when the sun wasn't shining?

A Lot to Learn

Eruç was not **bothered** by the hard work or even by being blown in the wrong direction. He sees the world as a **laboratory** where there is much to learn.

For example, he has learned from the birds that visit him on his boat at sea. If he sees **frigatebirds or noddy terns,** he knows that an island can't be far. These birds always return to the shore at the end of the day.

A friendly bird visits Eruç on his boat.

bothered upset
laboratory classroom
frigatebirds or noddy terns certain kinds of sea birds

▲ Eruç talks to a group of Girl Scouts in the Philippines about achieving goals in life.

Sharing His Story

On his adventure, Eruç stopped from time to time to visit with people on land. He enjoyed meeting everyone—especially all the students. He shared his story with **dozens of** schools.

Even today, Eruç **encourages** all kids to **set their eyes on** a goal and not give up. Like his experience in the Pacific Ocean, it may be challenging.

"If you don't try, you don't (or won't) go anywhere," Eruç says. "With goals, we will **make progress**. We will be farther along than when we started, even if we don't reach some goals. That's called life!" ❖

dozens of many
encourages tells
set their eyes on make
make progress learn and grow

Before You Continue

1. **Draw Conclusions** Eruç sees the world as a place to learn. What does this tell you about him?
2. **Main Idea** What does Eruç believe about goals?

PART 2 Think and Respond

Talk About It

Key Words	
challenge	explore
continent	globe
destination	journey
discover	location
endurance	prepare

1. What part of this **human interest feature** did you enjoy the most?

   I enjoyed the part ____.

2. Imagine that you are Eruç. Someone asks you why you want to row across the Pacific Ocean. **Express intentions** about your goal.

   I want to ____. I am going to ____.

3. Look at the map legend on page 275. How does it help you understand each part of Eruç's **journey**?

   The legend shows ____.

Write About It

Write a letter to Erden Eruç. Tell him what you think about his adventure. End your letter by telling him about a place you would like to **explore**. Use **Key Words**.

____, 20____

Dear Erden,

I just read an article about your trip around the world. I think ____.

Reread and Summarize

Main Idea and Details

Make a main idea diagram for different sections of "One Man's Goal." Base your main ideas on the section headings.

Main Idea Diagram

Main Idea	Details
Eruç decided to travel around the world.	He left California in a boat in 2007.
	He rowed across the Pacific Ocean to Australia.

Work with a partner. Use your diagrams to summarize different sections of "One Man's Goal." Use the sentence frames and **Key Words**. Record your summaries.

The main idea is ______. A detail that supports this is ______.

Fluency

Practice reading with phrasing. Rate your reading.

Talk Together

Look at the maps on pages 275 and 277. Pretend that you are Erden. Tell a partner how the maps helped you achieve your goal. Use **Key Words**.

Homographs

Homographs are words that have the same spelling but different meanings. Some homographs have different pronunciations, too. You can use context to figure out the correct meanings.

Train is a homograph. Compare the examples.

They **train** (/'tɹeɪn/) for a race.
Meaning: to practice for something

The **train** (/'tɹeɪn/) travels very fast.
Meaning: a line of railway cars on a track

Try It Together

Read the sentences. Then answer the questions.

A cold wind blows in my face as I sail my boat. I wind a scarf around my neck to keep me warm.

1. What does wind mean in the first sentence?

A a machine
B a kind of fish
C air that moves
D water that rises

2. What does wind mean in the second sentence?

A to sail a boat
B to stay warm
C to put on a hat
D to wrap around

Making Connections Read about another adventurer who **explores** places around the world.

Genre A **profile** is nonfiction. It gives facts about a person and his or her life.

Climbing Toward Her Goal

by **Guadalupe López**

Constanza Ceruti

Constanza Ceruti loves mountains and learning about **ancient civilizations**. As **a high-altitude archaeologist**, she climbs to the tops of mountains to **explore** **worship sites**. So far, she has climbed more than 100 mountains over 16,500 feet high.

ancient civilizations people who lived very long ago

a high-altitude archaeologist someone who studies old objects found on mountains

worship sites places where people used to pray

Before You Continue

1. **Make Inferences** Why did Ceruti become a high-altitude archaeologist?
2. **Main Idea and Details** Which details in the text support the idea that Ceruti loves history?

The Children of Llullaillaco

In 1999, Ceruti and her team climbed Llullaillaco, a mountain in Argentina. It was a harsh climb, with blowing snow, strong winds, and **low oxygen levels**.

SOUTH AMERICA

ARGENTINA

When the explorers finally reached the top, they found three frozen **Incan mummies**. Two girls and a boy were buried 500 years ago. The mummies still have hair on their arms, which makes them the best-preserved mummies in the world. The explorers also found gold and silver statues, **textiles**, and pottery.

"This was not just an archaeological find," says Ceruti. "This was like meeting someone from the ancient past."

Ceruti found objects buried with the mummies.

low oxygen levels very little air to breathe

Incan mummies preserved bodies from a group of people who lived long ago

textiles cloth

What the Explorers Found

▲ dish shaped like a duck

◀ wool bag

◀ gold statue

statue of a llama made from a shell ▶

▲ objects found buried with the mummies

▸ Before You Continue

1. **Ask Questions** What question did you ask yourself about the text? Tell a partner how you found the answer.
2. **Form Generalizations** What can you say about the objects the explorers found?

Paving the Path

Growing up in Argentina, Ceruti was always interested in ancient civilizations. Her dream was to live and work near the mountains. In school, Ceruti worked hard to reach her goal. Math was a subject she really had to **conquer**!

Now, Ceruti uses math all the time. "How many feet will we climb? How long will it take? What time do we start?" She knows that careful planning can mean the difference between **success and failure**.

Ceruti brushes dirt off a mummy.

Paving the Path Making a Plan
conquer work hard at to learn
success and failure a good trip or a bad trip

The **journey** to the top of Mount Llullaillaco was long and hard, but that did not stop Ceruti from climbing.

"Just think of the Incas who climbed these mountains hundreds of years ago," she says. "They **endured** the same conditions."

With **preparation** and **determination**, Ceruti proves one thing: no mountain—or goal—is too big to conquer! ❖

Ceruti climbed the same mountains the Incas did.

endured lived through
preparation good planning
determination courage

Before You Continue

1. **Summarize** What are the most important ideas in the text under "Paving the Path" on page 288?
2. **Analyze** Describe Ceruti's goal. Do you think she achieved it? Why or why not?

Key Words	
challenge	explore
continent	globe
destination	journey
discover	location
endurance	prepare

Compare Causes

Both Erden Eruç and Constanza Ceruti like physical **challenges**. What else causes them to do adventurous things? How are their reasons alike? How are they different? Work with a partner to complete a Venn diagram.

Venn Diagram

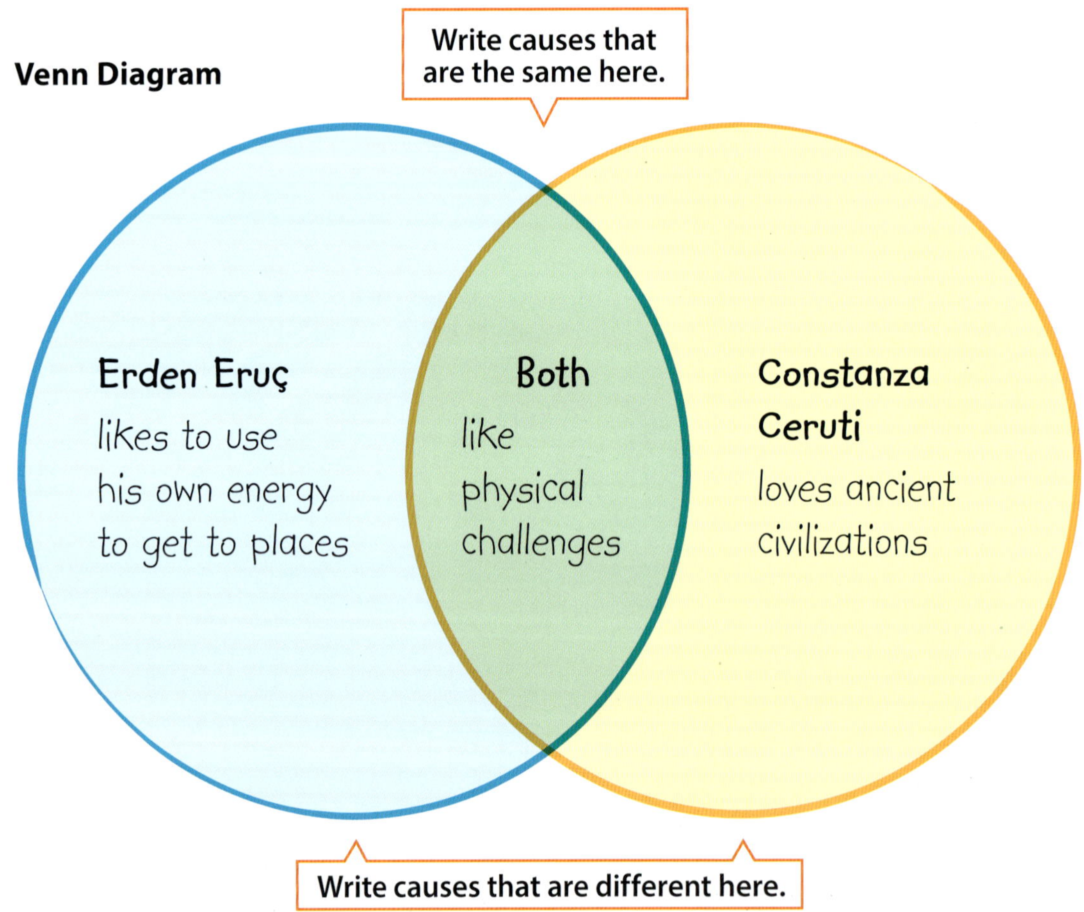

Talk Together

What tools can help people reach their goals? Think about the feature and the profile. Use **Key Words** to talk about your ideas.

Future Tense

There are two ways to show the **future tense**.

Grammar Rules Future Tense

	Now	In the Future
• Use the helping verb **will** along with a **main verb**.	**leave**	We **will leave** on a trip tomorrow.
• Use **am going to**, **are going to**, or **is going to** before a **main verb**.	**look**	I **am going to look** at a map later.
	ride	My friends **are going to ride** their bikes to my house.
	hike	Randy **is going to hike** up the mountain on Saturday.

Read in the Future Tense

Read these sentences about a journey. Can you find two examples of the future tense? Show them to a partner.

> My cousins are going to travel around the world. They will row a boat much of the way.

Write in the Future Tense

What do you think will happen to the cousins on their trip? Write a paragraph for your partner. Use the future tense.

Writing Project

Write as a Storyteller

Write a Story 

Write a story about someone who accomplishes an important goal. Share your story with the class. Make a collection of the class's short stories.

Study a Model

When you write a story, you create characters, a setting, and a plot. The plot often has a problem that the main character solves.

The beginning introduces the **main character**, the **setting**, and the **problem**.

Super Chicken!

by Devon Samuels

Marvin stood at the edge of the diving board. Every week, he climbed up the ladder of the high dive. Then, every week, he went right back down again. **The kids at the pool called him Super Chicken.**

Marvin looked down at the water. No way was he only three meters up! The pool people must have measured wrong.

"Jump!" some kids yelled.

Marvin counted to ten, which always made him calm, and sprang off the board. He hit the water with a big splash. When he came up, everyone cheered. He grinned. No more Super Chicken!

The writing has a clear voice and style. The writer uses words that show who he is.

The ending shows how the character solves the problem.

Prewrite

1. **Choose a Topic** What will your story be about? Talk with a partner to come up with ideas.

Language Frames

Tell Your Ideas	Respond to Ideas
• I think ______ would be interesting. • A story about ______ would be ______. • ______ would make a great ______ for my story.	• I like that idea because ______. • The main character should be someone who ______. • A better ______ might be ______.

2. **Gather Information** Who will your main character be? What is the person's goal? Write down your ideas.

3. **Get Organized** Use a story map to help you organize the events.

Story Map

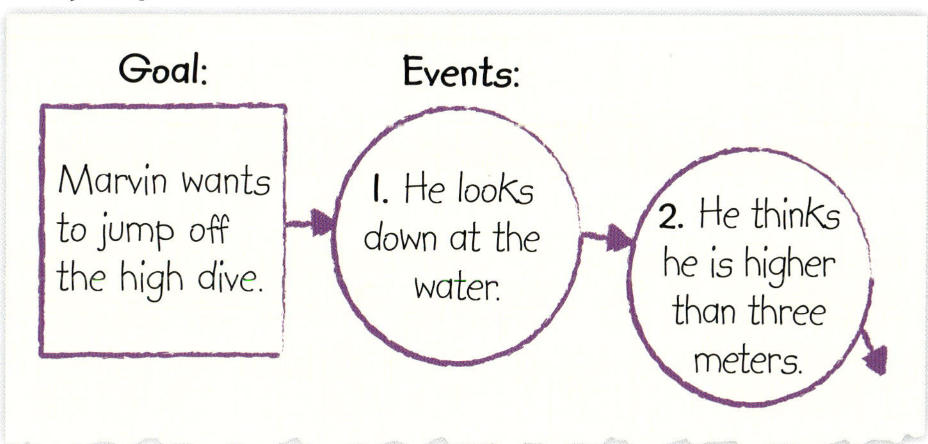

Draft

Write your first paragraph. Then use your story map to guide the rest of your draft. Use words that show who you are.

Writing Project, continued

Revise

1. **Read, Retell, Respond** Read your draft aloud to a partner. Your partner listens and then retells the story. Next, talk about ways to improve your writing.

Language Frames	
Retell	**Make Suggestions**
• The story is about ______. • It takes place ______. • The first thing that happens is ______.	• I like the story, but I'm confused about where it happens. Is the setting ______? • This story doesn't show who you are. You should use words that ______.

2. **Make Changes** Think about your draft and your partner's suggestions. Then use revision marks to make your changes.

   - Make sure your readers know where your story takes place.

     at the pool
     The kids called him Super Chicken.

   - Do your words and sentences sound like you? If not, make revisions.

     No way was he
     ~~He couldn't believe he was~~ only three meters up!

Edit and Proofread

Work with a partner to edit and proofread your story. Check verbs in the past tense. Use revision marks to show your changes.

Spelling Tip

For most regular verbs, add -**ed** to show past tense. For some regular verbs, change the base word before you add -**ed**.

Present

1. **On Your Own** Make a final copy of your story. Read it aloud to a younger or older friend or to family members. Tell them how you got your ideas.

Presentation Tips	
If you are the speaker...	**If you are the listener...**
Use gestures to help your listeners imagine what is happening in the story.	Listen attentively and picture the events in the story.
If you tell your story to younger children, retell it with simpler words and sentences.	Think about what lesson you could learn from the story.

2. **With a Group** Make a short story collection. Put all of your class's stories in a book or post them online. Think of a title that lets readers know that the stories are about goals.

Talk Together

In this unit, you found lots of answers to the **Big Question**. Now, use your concept map to discuss the **Big Question** with the class.

Concept Map

Write a Story 

Choose a tool for success from your concept map. Write a story about someone who used the tool to reach a goal.

Unit 8 **Wrap-Up**

Share Your Ideas

Choose one of these ways to share your ideas about the **Big Question**.

Talk About It!

Talk Show

Work with two classmates. Pretend you are on a TV talk show. One person is the host. The other two are the guests. Discuss tools you use to achieve goals at home and at school.

Write It!

Plan a Trip

Work with a partner. Pretend you are going on a camping trip. Make a list of information, such as how much food you will need, how far your destination is, and how far you will travel each day.

Do It!

Guessing Game

Work with a small group to play a guessing game. Take turns. Pantomime something you have to use numbers to do, such as make a recipe or keep score for a game. Other classmates guess your actions.

Write It!

Make a Map

Imagine a place you would like to visit. Draw a map. Show how to get there from your home. Put distances and other information on your map. Share it with a partner.

Picture Dictionary

The definitions are for the words as they are introduced in the selections of this book.

Parts of an Entry

A

achieve
verb
To **achieve** means to get something that you work for.

*She worked hard to **achieve** first place.*

alter
verb
When you **alter** something, you change it.

*She **alters** the dress to make it shorter.*

area
noun
An **area** is a part of a place.

*A classroom can have an **area** for reading.*

artist
noun
An **artist** is someone who is skilled at drawing, painting, making things, or performing.

*This **artist** paints what she sees outdoors.*

C

carve
verb
To **carve** is to make something by cutting.

*Dad **carves** the pumpkin while I watch.*

challenge
noun
A **challenge** is something that is hard to do.

*It is a **challenge** to climb up a rope.*

combine
verb
When you **combine** things, you mix them together.

*What foods does she **combine**?*

communicate
verb
When you **communicate**, you share words or feelings.

*She **communicates** with a friend.*

a b c d e f g h i j k l m n o p q r s t u v w x y z

composition

noun

Composition is what things are made of.

*The **composition** of mud is dirt and water.*

continent

noun

A **continent** is one of the major divisions of land on Earth.

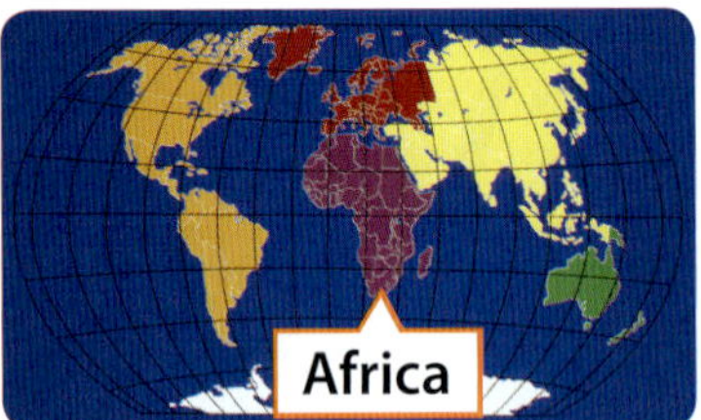

*Africa is one of seven **continents**.*

core

noun

The **core** is the middle of something.

*An apple **core** is the center part of an apple.*

create

verb

To **create** means to make something new.

*She **creates** a picture.*

destination

noun

A **destination** is the place you are traveling to.

*They look for their **destination** on a map.*

develop

verb

When something **develops**, it grows over time.

*The small plant will **develop** into a large tree.*

direction

noun

When you move toward something, you move in that **direction**.

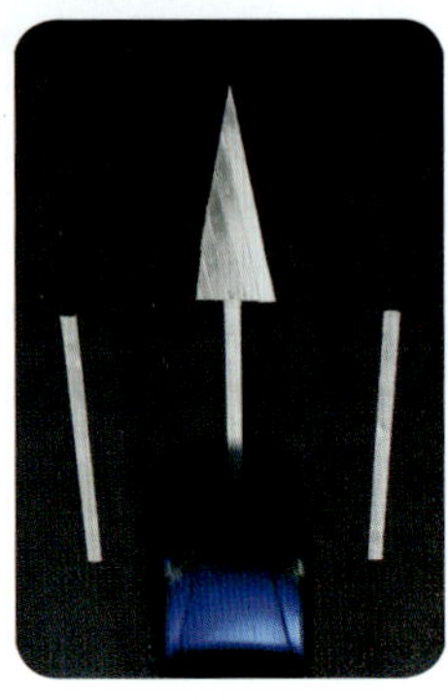

*The arrow shows the **direction** of the road.*

discover

verb

When you **discover** something, you find it.

*She **discovers** an insect on this plant.*

distance

noun

The **distance** is the amount of space between two places.

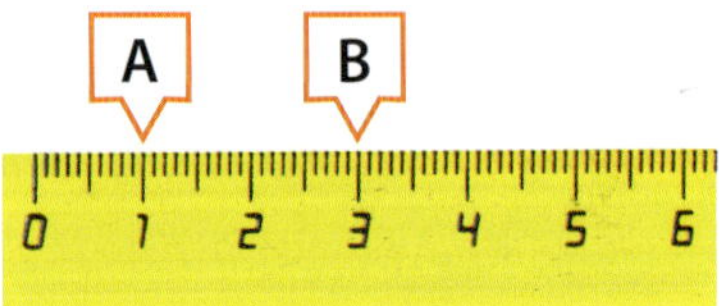

*The **distance** between A and B is two inches.*

E

earthquake

noun

An **earthquake** is a sudden violent shaking of Earth that may cause damage.

*An **earthquake** damaged this building.*

endurance

noun

When you have **endurance**, you keep doing something.

*A long race takes **endurance**.*

erupt

verb

When a volcano **erupts,** it throws out smoke, rocks, hot ashes, and lava.

*It is dangerous to be nearby when a volcano **erupts**!*

estimate

verb

When you make a guess about something, you **estimate**.

*Can you **estimate** how many coins are in the jar?*

explore

verb

To **explore** means to go somewhere to learn about people or things.

*He **explores** a new area.*

express

verb

To **express** a thought or an emotion is to say or show it.

*She **expresses** her love for her baby.*

F

feelings

noun

Feelings are how you experience something.

*Happiness and surprise are kinds of **feelings**.*

feet

noun

Feet are units of length. One foot is twelve inches long.

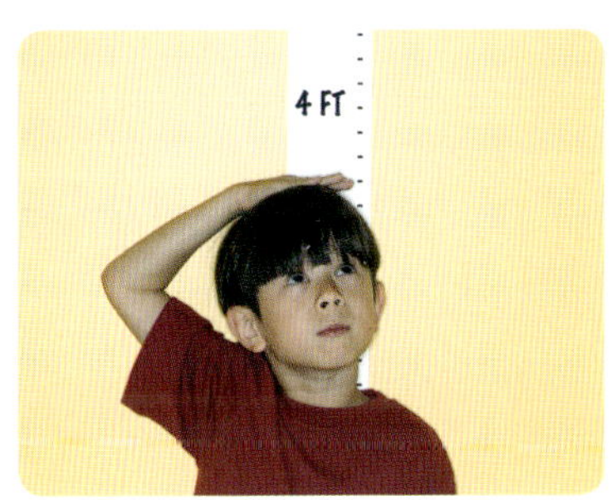

*He is almost four **feet** tall.*

firm

adjective

Something that is **firm** is hard.

*You can skate on ice because it is **firm**.*

a b c d e f g h i j k l m n o p q r s t u v w x y z

flow

verb

To **flow** means to move along smoothly.

*The ice cream **flows** from the machine into the cone.*

force

noun

Force means power or strength.

*The **force** of the wind bends this tree.*

form

noun

A **form** is a distinct state of matter.

*Steam is one **form** of water.*

freeze

verb

To **freeze** is to become solid or icy at a very low temperature.

*We **freeze** water to make ice cubes for iced tea.*

G

generation

noun

A **generation** is made up of people born around the same year.

*They are in different **generations**.*

globe

noun

A **globe** is a sphere with a map of the world on it.

*We can locate different places on the **globe**.*

goal

noun

A **goal** is something that you want to do.

*His **goal** is to catch the ball.*

ground

noun

Ground, or land, is the solid part of Earth's surface.

*He plants flowers in the **ground**.*

H

heritage

noun

Your **heritage** is the traditions, ideas, and language of your ancestors.

*People of Mexican **heritage** celebrate Cinco de Mayo.*

I

island

noun

An **island** is a piece of land completely surrounded by water.

*This **island** is in the Caribbean Sea.*

J

journey

noun

A **journey** is a long trip.

*Horses pulled covered wagons in the long, hard **journey** west.*

K

kilometer

noun

A **kilometer** is a unit of measurement. Its length equals 1,000 meters.

*The Golden Gate Bridge is about 3 **kilometers** long.*

L

lava

noun

Lava is the hot, liquid rock that comes out of a volcano when it erupts.

*The **lava** flows from the volcano's crater.*

liquid

adjective

Something that is **liquid** can be poured.

*Milk is a **liquid** substance.*

location

noun

A **location** is a place or a position.

*This is a good **location** for looking at the clouds.*

M

magma

noun

Magma is melted rock found beneath Earth's surface.

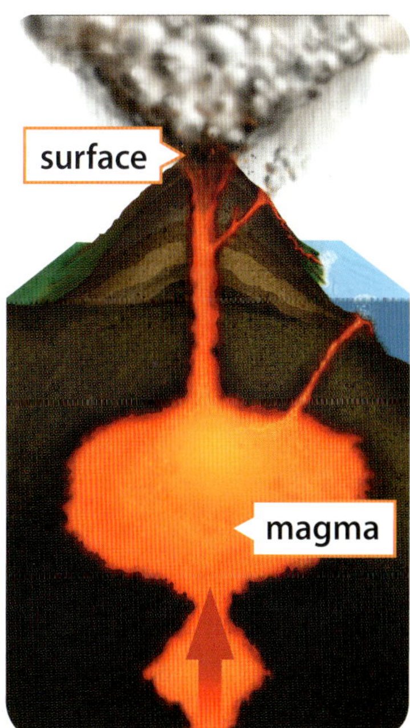

***Magma** becomes lava when it flows out of a volcano.*

measurement
noun

Measurement is the process of finding out the size, weight, or amount of something.

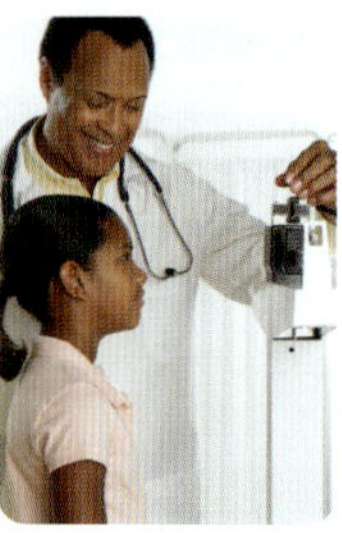

*This scale is for the **measurement** of body weight.*

melt
verb

When something **melts**, it changes from a solid to a liquid.

*Ice cream **melts** quickly.*

meter
noun

A **meter** is the basic unit of measurement in the metric system. It is equal to about three feet.

*A baseball bat is about one **meter** long.*

mixture
noun

A **mixture** is something made by combining different things together.

*Add flour to this cake **mixture**.*

music
noun

Music is a pleasing group of sounds.

*She make **music** with this instrument.*

O

occur
verb

When something **occurs**, it happens.

*A sunrise **occurs** every morning.*

ocean
noun

The **ocean** is the large amount of salt water that covers most of Earth's surface.

*The blue area on the globe shows the different **oceans**.*

P

perform
verb

When you **perform**, you put on a show for a group of people.

*The girls **perform** on stage.*

*A mariachi band **performs** in a plaza in Mexico.*

plate
noun
A **plate** is one of many sheets of rock that make up Earth's outer crust.

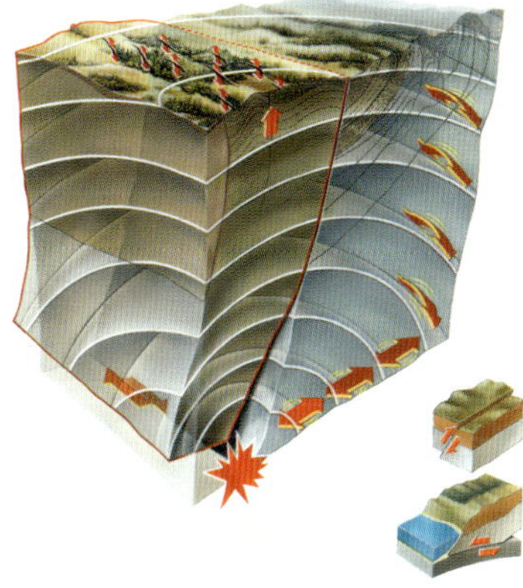

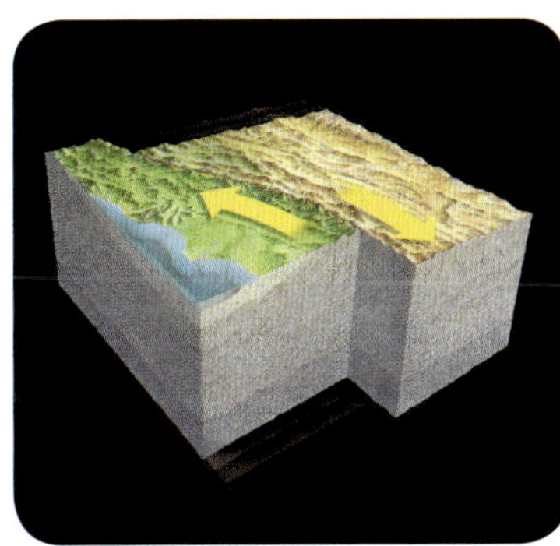

*Moving **plates** can cause an earthquake.*

popular
adjective
When many people like a place or a thing, it is **popular**.

*This restaurant is **popular**.*

power
noun
If something has **power**, it is strong.

*Strong waves have the **power** to destroy a building.*

prepare
verb
To **prepare** means to get ready for something.

*She packs a suitcase to **prepare** for her trip.*

preservation
noun
Preservation is the act of keeping something safe for a long time.

*The **preservation** of old documents is important.*

pressure
noun
When one thing pushes against another, it makes **pressure**.

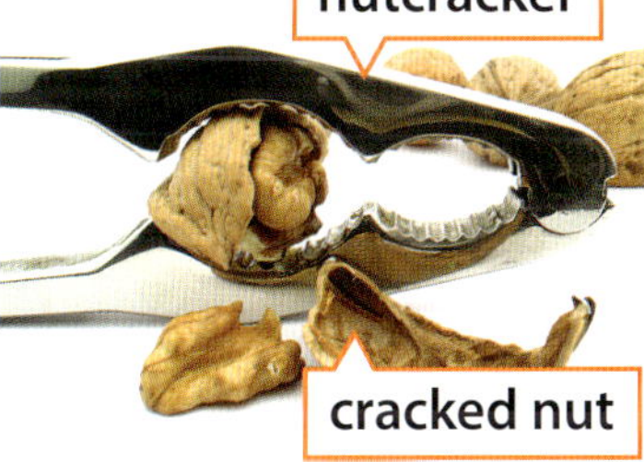

***Pressure** from the nutcracker causes the nuts to crack open.*

process
noun
When you follow a **process**, you do something step by step.

*He follows a **process** to put the model together.*

a b c d e f g h i j k l m n o p q r s t u v w x y z

R

region

noun

A **region** is an area.

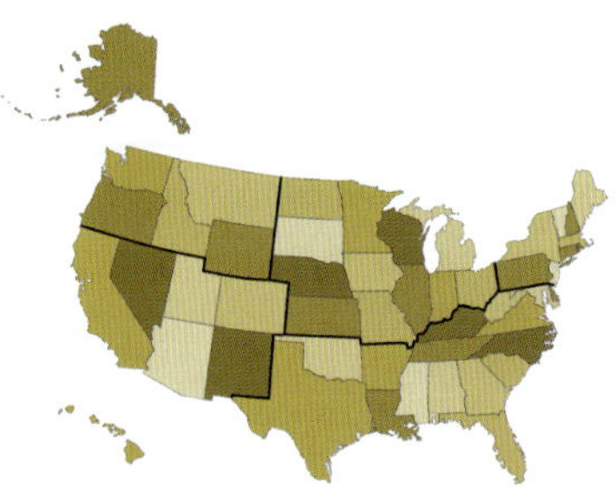

*There are many **regions** in the United States.*

represent

verb

To **represent** means to stand for.

*A heart **represents** love.*

rescue

verb

When you **rescue** someone, you save the person.

*A dog helps to **rescue** a skier.*

rescue (continued)

*A fireman **rescues** a girl from a burning building.*

rhythm

noun

Rhythm is a regular, repeated beat in music, poetry, or dance.

*This drummer keeps the **rhythm** of the song.*

rock

noun

A **rock** is a piece of stone.

*She is holding a **rock**.*

S

sand

noun

Sand is very tiny pieces of rock that make up beaches and deserts.

*It is fun to play in the **sand**.*

sense

verb

When you **sense** something, you know it without being told.

*A cat can **sense** danger.*

shore
noun
The **shore** is the land at the edge of an ocean, a river, or a lake.

*Seashells wash up on the **shore**.*

signal
noun
A **signal** is something that tells you what to do.

*The green light is a **signal** to walk.*

*The red light is a **signal** to stop.*

solid
adjective
Something that is **solid** is firm.

*The chair is **solid**. You can sit on it.*

*The sidewalk is **solid**. You can stand on it.*

state
noun
The **state** of a person or thing is the way it is at a certain time.

*He is in a happy **state**.*

state (continued)

*She is in a sad **state**.*

storyteller
noun
A **storyteller** tells tales to entertain people.

*The children listen to the **storyteller**.*

strategy
noun
A **strategy** is a plan for success.

*She has a **strategy** for winning.*

style

noun

Style is a way of doing something.

*He paints in a colorful **style**.*

substance

noun

Substance is the material something is made of.

*Snow is a cold **substance**.*

surface

noun

A **surface** is the outside part of something.

*The **surface** of this ball is bumpy.*

surface (continued)

*The **surface** of this watermelon is smooth.*

T

tale

noun

A **tale** is a story about things that are made up.

Making Connections Read more about how our actions today can affect the **future**.

Genre A **fable** is a story that teaches a lesson, or moral, about life. Many fables have animals as characters.

The Ant and the Grasshopper

an Aesop fable

retold by **Shirleyann Costigan**
illustrated by **Pablo Bernasconi**

One sunny day, a **merry** grasshopper was dancing to his fiddle. "**Watch your step!**" came a voice at his feet. It was an ant carrying **an enormous kernel** of corn.

merry happy
"Watch your step!" "Be careful where you walk!"
an enormous kernel a big piece

Before You Continue

1. **Ask Questions** What do you want to find out as you read? If you don't understand something, what will you do?
2. **Character** What is the grasshopper like? How do you know?

TURTLE AND HIS FOUR COUSINS

a Cuban folk tale retold by **Margaret Read MacDonald**
Illustrated by **Raúl Colón**

"Hey, Slow Poke Turtle! Move those little legs!" called Deer. Deer made fun of other creatures. Turtle didn't care.

"Slow Poke yourself! I am faster than you," he **muttered**.

"Ha!" snorted Deer. "Look at my long legs! Want to RACE?"

Turtle stopped. "Hmm, I wonder . . ." he mumbled. Then he had an idea. "Meet me tomorrow at the beach. We will race all the way to the fourth hill."

Deer ran off laughing. "Tomorrow you LOSE!" he called.

muttered said quietly

*Children enjoy reading folk **tales**.*

temperature

noun

The **temperature** of something is how hot or cold it is.

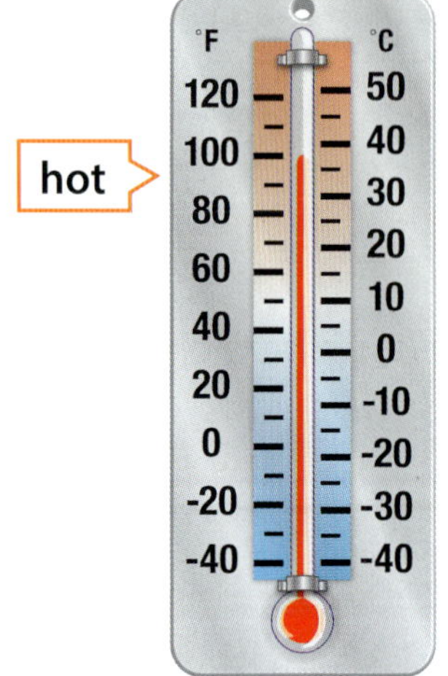

*The **temperature** is hot.*

*The **temperature** outside is very cold.*

thermometer

noun

A **thermometer** is used to measure temperature.

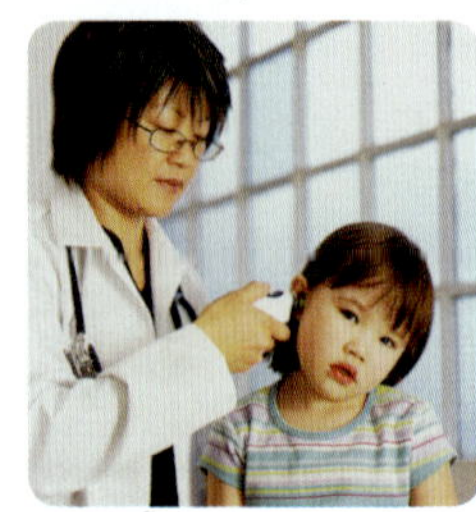

*The doctor uses a **thermometer** to check for a fever.*

tradition

noun

A **tradition** is something that people have done for a long time and continue to do.

***Traditions** are important to many families.*

trap

verb

To **trap** something means to catch it and not let it go.

*Spiders **trap** insects with webs.*

tsunami

noun

A **tsunami** is a huge, dangerous, ocean wave. Underwater earthquakes cause tsunamis.

*The **tsunami** crashes into buildings and floods the city.*

unit

noun

A **unit** is an amount used in measuring or counting.

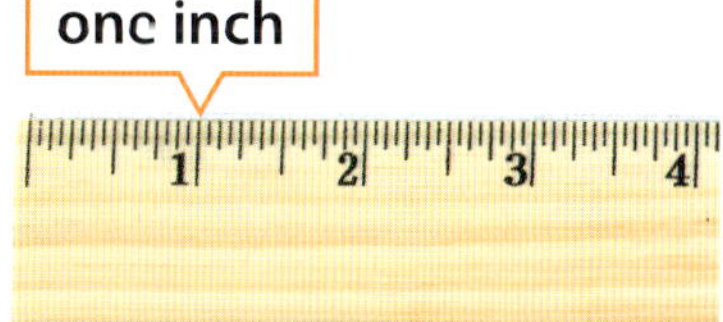

*An inch is a **unit** of length.*

vary

verb

To **vary** something is to change it often.

vary (continued)

*I like to **vary** my lunches.*

volcano

noun

A **volcano** is a mountain that can erupt. It has a large hole at the top called a crater. When a volcano erupts it shoots out hot lava, burning rocks, ash, and hot gases.

*This **volcano** is erupting.*

a b c d e f g h i j k l m n o p q r s t u v w x y z

a b c d e f g h i j k l m n o p q r s t u v w x y z

W

warn

verb

To **warn** people is to tell them that something bad may happen.

*She **warns** people to stop.*

water

noun

Water is a clear liquid that you can drink or use to wash with.

***Water** falls from the sky and fills oceans, lakes, and rivers.*

wave

noun

A **wave** is a vibration through the air or water.

*The computer records a sound **wave**.*

wave (continued)

*The **wave** is crashing on the beach.*

wetland

noun

A **wetland** is a place where there is a lot of moisture or water in the soil.

***Wetland** ecosystems are a habitat for many kinds of plants and animals.*

*Many plants grow in a **wetland**.*

wood

noun

Wood is the hard material that tree trunks and branches are made of.

*He is cutting the tree so people can use its **wood**.*

*This man is making a table from **wood**.*

Index

D

E

F

G

N

O

P

W

Index of Authors

Index of Illustrators

Index of Photographers

Text and Illustrator Credits

Unit Five

Excerpt from "Quicksand" by Kris Hirschmann. Published in 2002 by Gale, an imprint of Cengage Learning, Inc.

Unit Six

Highlights for Children: Excerpt from "Carving Stones in Cedar" by Kristine F. Anderson from Highlights for Children, November 2007. Copyright © 2007 by Highlights for Children. Reprinted by permission of Highlights for Children, Inc.

Unit Seven

HarperCollins Publishers: Excerpt from "An Island Grows" by Lola M. Schaefer, Illustrated by Cathie Felstead. Text copyright © 2006 by Lola M. Schaefer. Illustrations © 2006 by Cathie Felstead. Used by permission of HarperCollins Publishers.

LEE & LOW BOOKS, Inc: From "Selvakumar Knew Better" by Virginia Kroll, illustrated by Xiaojun Li. Text copyright © 2006 by Virginia Kroll, Illustrations © 2006 by Xiaojun Li. Permission arranged with Shen's Books, an imprint of LEE & LOW BOOKS, Inc., New York, NY 10016. All rights not specifically granted herein are reserved.

Unit Eight

Excerpt from "Running Shoes" by Frederick Lipp, illustrated by Jason Gaillard. Text copyright © 2007 by Frederick Lipp. Illustrations © 2007 by Jason Gaillard. Text and illustrations reproduced with kind permission of Frederick Lipp and Jason Gaillard.

Photographic Credits

Cover C. Haessler/Shutterstock.com. iii (tl) SHAH MARAI/Getty Images (tr) ABRAHAM NOWITZ / National Geographic Image Collection (bl) Philippe Bourseiller/The Image Bank/Getty Images (br) Johner Images/Getty Images. v Arne Hodalic/ Corbis/Getty Images. ix TORU YAMANAKA/AFP/ Getty Images. xi TERRY SCHMITT/UPI/Newscom. 2–3 SHAH MARAI/Getty Images. 7 (tl) ugurhan/ iStock/Getty Images (tc) IakovKalinin/iStock/Getty Images (tr) Comstock/Stockbyte/Getty Images (bl) Elena Elisseeva/Shutterstock.com (bc) LionH/E+/ Getty Images. 10 (tl) Fotokostic/Shutterstock.com (tr) Fotokostic/Shutterstock.com (cl) Kobby Dagan/ Shutterstock.com (cr) V J Matthew/Shutterstock. com (bl) Triple D Studio/Shutterstock.com (br) Rawpixel.com/Shutterstock.com. 11 Tyler Olson/Shutterstock.com. 31 (bkgd) Arne Hodalic/ Corbis/Getty Images (inset) National Geographic Image Collection. 32–33 Poorfish/Moment/Getty Images. 33 (r) AP Images/NTV, Russian Television Channel. 34–35 Poorfish/Moment/Getty Images. 34 (r) International Mammoth Committee/National Geographic Image Collection. 35 (t) International Mammoth Committee/National Geographic Image Collection (br) International Mammoth Committee/National Geographic Image Collection. 38 Nickolya/Shutterstock.com. 41 (tl) Ryan McVay/ Photodisc/Getty Images (tc) RapidEye/E+/Getty Images (tr) AnnaDudek/iStock/Getty Images (bl) RichLegg/E+/Getty Images (bc) Thomas Northcut/Photodisc/Getty Images. 42 Joseph Devenney/Getty Images. 44 (l) Francesco Scatena/ Shutterstock.com (r) Orla/Shutterstock.com. 45 Daniel Korzeniewski/Shutterstock.com. 46–47 Roland Liptak/Alamy Stock Photo. 48 (l) Bettmann/Getty Images (r) Everett Collection. 49 pio3/Shutterstock.com. 50 Gallo Images/Alamy Stock Photo. 51 (l) Harald Sund/Getty Images (r) Alexander Walter/Getty Images. 52 Jupiterimages/ Getty Images. 54–55 Winfield Parks/National Geographic Image Collection. 55 (r) Giorgio Fochesato/Getty Images. 56–57 Arlene Treiber Waller/Shutterstock.com. 58 Bettmann/Getty Images. 60 kozmoat98/Getty Images. 61 (bkgd) Jim Zuckerman/Getty Images (inset) Dr. Maycira Costa. 62–63 Panoramic Images/National Geographic Image Collection. 62 (t) Joseph H. Bailey/National Geographic Image Collection (tr) Nature and Science/Alamy Stock Photo (tcr) Semmick Photo/ Shutterstock.com (bcr) Michael Nichols/National Geographic Image Collection (br) Panoramic Images/National Geographic Image Collection. 63 (tr) Luciano Candisani/Minden Pictures (tcr) Luciano Candisani/Minden Pictures (bcr) Bates Littlehales/National Geographic Image Collection (br) Gerry Ellis/Minden Pictures. 64–65 JOEL SARTORE/National Geographic Image Collection. 64 (bl) Dr. Maycira Costa (tr) Planet Observer/ Getty Images. 65 Jim Sugar/Corbis Documentary/ Getty Images. 72 SHAH MARAI/Getty Images. 73 (tr) vasabii/Shutterstock.com (bl) valzan/ Shutterstock.com (br) Mega Pixel/Shutterstock. com. 75–75 ABRAHAM NOWITZ /National Geographic Image Collection. 77 (tl) Alija/Getty Images (tr) WILLIAM ALBERT ALLARD/National Geographic Image Collection (b) Bob Krist/Corbis Documentary/Getty Images. 78 Masterfile. 79 (tl) kate_sept2004/Getty Images (tc) creativepictures/ iStock/Getty Images (tr) Sean De Burca/Taxi/Getty Images (bl) Filipe Frazao/Shutterstock.com (bc) Sami Sarkis/Getty Images. 82 (tl) Hutsuliak Dmytro/Shutterstock.com (tr) Maridav/ Shutterstock.com (cl) wavebreakmedia/ Shutterstock.com (cr) Daxiao Productions/ Shutterstock.com (bl) Africa Studio/Shutterstock. com (br) EvGavrilov/Shutterstock.com. 83 ChameleonsEye/Shutterstock.com. 97 The Photo Access/Alamy Stock Photo. 101–105 PrimaStockPhoto/Shutterstock.com. 101 (br) Hulton Archive/Getty Images. 102 (tr) The Granger Collection, Ltd. (bl) Schwabenblitz/Shutterstock. com. 103 (b) Mara Vivat/Getty Images. 104 (cl) GAB Archive/Redferns/Getty Images (cr) Colin Underhill/Alamy Stock Photo. 105 (l) John Shearer/ Getty Images (c) Bernd Mueller/Getty Images (r) Jon Super/Getty Images. 109 (tl) Historical/Corbis Historical/Getty Images (tr) Jeff Haynes/Getty Images (bl) Alinari Archives/Getty Images (br) David Grossman/Alamy Stock Photo. 111 (tl) MBI/ Alamy Stock Photo (tc) OMG/Stockbyte/Getty Images (tr) bonniej/iStock/Getty Images (bl) David Papazian/Corbis/Getty Images (bc) Dmitriy Shironosov/Alamy Stock Photo. 114 (tl) Michelle D. Milliman/Shutterstock.com (tr) A3pfamily/ Shutterstock.com. 115 Todor Rusinov/Shutterstock. com. 116–117 University of Washington Libraries, Special Collections. 116 (inset) SCPhotos/Alamy Stock Photo. 117 SCPhotos/Alamy Stock Photo. 118–119 Joseph Sohm/amana images/Getty Images. 119 (r) John Elk/Lonely Planet Images/Getty Images. 120–121 Joseph Sohm/amana images/ Getty 120 (inset) Shotridge Studios. 121 (tr) Gary Warnimont/Alamy Stock Photo (bl) Shotridge Studios (br) Shotridge Studios. 122–23 Akira Kaede/Getty Images. 122 (inset) Shotridge Studios. 123 (tr) Shotridge Studios (bl) Shotridge Studios (br) Shotridge Studios. 124–125 Melissa Farlow/ National Geographic Image Collection. 125 (tr) Danita Delimont/Getty Images. 126 Shotridge Studios. 128 (bc) PHOTOPLAY/DIGITAL VISION/ Media Bakery. 130 Shotridge Studios. 133 Elizabeth Lindsey. 134 (bkgd) DIANE COOK, LEN JENSHEL/National Geographic Image Collection (inset) Adam Jones/Visuals Unlimited, Inc. 135 Elizabeth Lindsey. 141 (l) Brand X Pictures/Getty Images (r) Jacobs Stock Photography/Getty Images. 146 ABRAHAM NOWITZ /National Geographic Image Collection. 148–149 Philippe Bourseiller/ The Image Bank/Getty Images. 151 Philippe Bourseiller/The Image Bank/Getty Images. 153 (tl) FoodCollection/Superstock (tc) Ariel Skelley/ DigitalVision/Getty Images (tr) Stuart O'Sullivan/ The Image Bank/Getty Images (bl) underworld/ Shutterstock.com (br) Goos_Lar/iStock/Getty Images. 154 mikeuk/Getty Images. 156 (tl) Dmitry Kalinovsky/Shutterstock.com (c) fboudrias/ Shutterstock.com (tr) MIA Studio/Shutterstock. com. 157 lara-sh/Shutterstock.com. 163 A.T. White/The Image Bank/Getty Images. 175 Carsten Peter/National Geographic Image Collection. 176–177 Carsten Peter/National Geographic Image Collection. 177 (l) Carsten Peter/National Geographic Image Collection (r) Carsten Peter/ National Geographic Image Collection. 178–179 Carsten Peter/National Geographic Image Collection. 178 (l) Carsten Peter/National Geographic Image Collection. 179 (inset) Carsten Peter/National Geographic Image Collection. 185 (tl) AP Images/MICHAEL DWYER (tc) Figure8Photos/E+/Getty Images (tr) Vera Zinkova/ Shutterstock.com (bl) John Foxx/Getty Images (bc) Lisa F. Young/Shutterstock.com. 186 China Daily CDIC/Reuters. 188 (l) 1xMaster/Shutterstock.com (c) sarawut panchawa/Shutterstock.com (r) Jo Ann Snover/Shutterstock.com. 189 TORU YAMANAKA/ AFP/Getty Images. 203 (tr) Xiaojun Li (bl) AP Images/CHRIS TOMLINSON. 206 (tl) Hkrunning | Dreamstime.com (tr) AlpamayoPhoto/Getty Images. 207 (inset) Willyam Bradberry/Shutterstock.com (bkgd) jarvis gray/Shutterstock.com. 209 Historical/Corbis Historical/Getty Images. 210 (c) Marco Garcia/Getty Images News/Getty Images. 216 Carsten Peter/National Geographic Image Collection. 220 (t) Philippe Bourseiller/The Image Bank/Getty Images (br) Colin Anderson/Getty Images. 222–223 Johner Images/Getty Images. 225 Lawrence Wee/Shutterstock.com. 227 (tl) Bruce Dale/National Geographic Image Collection (tc) YAY Media AS/Alamy Stock Photo (tr) Grace Clementine/Photodisc/Getty Images (bl) Brand X Pictures/Stockbyte/Getty Images (bc) Trofimova Vika/Shutterstock.com. 230 (tl) Sorbis/ Shutterstock.com (tr) MediaGroup_BestForYou/ Shutterstock.com. 231 Photoholgic/Shutterstock. com. 234 maxstockphoto/Shutterstock.com. 241 cobalt/iStockphoto.com. 247 Frederick Lipp. 262 kdshutterman/Shutterstock.com. 263 Brian Hagiwara/Stockbyte/Getty Images. 265 (tl) Richard Lewisohn/Photodisc/Getty Images (tc) Buena Vista Images/Stockbyte/Getty Images (tr) Alla Greeg/ Shutterstock.com (bl) Pavel Semenov/Shutterstock. com (bc) Eric Raptosh Photography/Stockbyte/ Getty Images. 267 (t) Donald R. Swartz/ Shutterstock.com (c) Rudi Von Briel/Photolibrary/ Getty Images (b) John Foxx/Stockbyte/Getty Images. 268 (tl) binik/Shutterstock.com (tc) Hurst Photo/Shutterstock.com (tr) Songquan Deng/ Shutterstock.com. 269 Billion Photos/Shutterstock. com. 270–271 TERRY SCHMITT/UPI/Newscom. 271 Brian Smale. 272 ERDEN ERUC/United Press International (UPI)/Newscom. 273 (t) SteveStone/ E+/Getty Images (c) Gary S Chapman/ Photographers Choice RF/Getty Images (b) Galyna Andrushko/Shutterstock.com. 274 Erden Eruç. 276 TERRY SCHMITT/UPI/Newscom. 278 (l) Erden Eruç (c) Erden Eruç (r) kenary820/ Shutterstock.com. 279 (c) Erden Eruç (br) StockPhotosArt - Objects/Alamy Stock Photo. 280 Erden Eruç. 281 Erden Eruç. 282 ERDEN ERUC/United Press International (UPI)/Newscom. 284 (l) maridav/Shutterstock.com (r) John Leung/ Shutterstock.com. 285 Constanza Ceruti. 286 Constanza Ceruti. 287 (tl) Stephen Alvarez/ National Geographic Image Collection (tr) DEA/G. DAGLI ORTI/Getty Images (cr) DEA/G. DAGLI ORTI/Getty Images (bl) JUAN MABROMATA/Getty Images (br) Stephen Alvarez/National Geographic Image Collection. 288 Constanza Ceruti. 289 Vadim Ozz/Shutterstock.com. 296 Johner Images/ Getty Images. 298 Ariel Skelley/DigitalVision/ Getty Images. 299 (tl) Bruce Dale/National Geographic Image Collection (tc) Chris Noble/ Photodisc/Getty Images (tr) Richard Lewisohn/ Photodisc/Getty Images (cl) ugurhan/iStock/Getty Images (c) Jupiterimages/Stockbyte/Getty Images (cr) RapidEye/E+/Getty Images (bl) Ryan McVay/ Photodisc/Getty Images (bc) Warut Chinsai/ Shutterstock.com (br) MBI/Alamy Stock Photo. 300 (tl) aniad/Shutterstock.com (tc) Ariel Skelley/ DigitalVision/Getty Images (tr) YAY Media AS/ Alamy Stock Photo (cl) A. Huber/U. Starke/Getty Images (c) Andersen Ross/Blend Images/Getty Images (cr) Buena Vista Images/Stockbyte/Getty Images (bl) Foodcollection/Getty Images (bc) Stuart O'Sullivan/The Image Bank/Getty Images (br) Andrey_Kuzmin/Shutterstock.com. 301 (tl) Everett Historical/Shutterstock.com (tc) Grace Clementine/Photodisc/Getty Images (tr) creativepictures/iStock/Getty Images (cl) Alla Greeg/Shutterstock.com (c) Pavel Semenov/ Shutterstock.com (cr) Randy Faris/Corbis/Getty Images (bl) Westend61/Masterfile (bc) kate_ sept2004/Getty Images (br) RichLegg/E+/Getty Images. 302 (tl) Joe Raedle/Getty Images News/ Getty Images (tc) HannamariaH/iStock/Getty Images (tr) Brand X Pictures/Stockbyte/Getty Images (cl) underworld/Shutterstock.com (c) OMG/ Stockbyte/Getty Images (cr) Leander Baerenz/ Photodisc/Getty Images (bl) sinelev/Shutterstock. com (bc) Ingram Publishing/Alamy Stock Photo (br) Stewart Cohen/Getty Images. 303 (tl) Drazen Vukelic/Shutterstock.com (tc) Stas Volik/ Shutterstock.com (tr) Galyna Andrushko/ Shutterstock.com (c) beboy/Shutterstock.com (bl) Jan Butchofsky/Getty Images (bc) Meiko Arquillos/ UpperCut Images/Getty Images (br) BSIP SA/Alamy Stock Photo. 304 (tl) Fuse/Corbis/Getty Images (tc) PhotoDisc/Stockbyte/Getty Images (tr) Ingram Publishing/Alamy Stock Photo (cl) moira lovell/ Alamy Stock Photo (c) Digital Vision/Getty Images (cr) Sean De Burca/Taxi/Getty Images (bl) bigjom jom/Shutterstock.com (bc) IakovKalinin/iStock/ Getty Images (br) Alija/Getty Images. 305 (tl) Richard Leech/Getty Images (tc) Xie Mingfei/VCG/ Getty Images (tr) bonniej/iStock/Getty Images (cl) Gary Hincks/Science Source (c) AP Images/ MICHAEL DWYER (cr) Goos_Lar/iStock/Getty Images (bl) Filipe Frazao/Shutterstock.com (bc) Eric Raptosh Photography/Stockbyte/Getty Image (br) David Papazian/Corbis/Getty Images. 306 (tl) Roman Sotola/Dreamstime.com (tc) JGI/Blend Images/Getty Image (tr) Robert McCann/age fotostock/Getty Images (cl) shironosov/iStock/ Getty Images (c) Photodisc/Getty Images (cr) Librakv/Dreamstime.com (bl) Figure8Photos/E+/ Getty Images (bc) 2windspa/E+/Getty Images (br) Vera Zinkova/Shutterstock.com. 307 (tl) michaeljung/Shutterstock.com (tc) FamVeld/ Shutterstock.com (tr) Blend Images/Superstock (cl) JOHN FOXX/Media Bakery (c) Paul Simcock/ Photodisc/Getty Images (cr) Chronicle/Alamy Ptock Photo (bl) Image Source/Getty Images (bc) Comstock/Stockbyte/Getty Images (br) Trofimova Vika/Shutterstock.com. 308 (tl) Sami Sarkis/Getty Images (tc) FOODCOLLECTION/Media Bakery (cl) Elena Elisseeva/Shutterstock.com (cr) Helga Fluey/Shutterstock.com (bl) Thomas Northcut/ Photodisc/Getty Images (br) Peter Dazeley/Getty Images. 309 (tl) Ariel Skelley/DigitalVision/Getty Images (tc) gmcoop/Getty Images (tr) Comstock Images/Stockbyte/Getty Images (cl) David Young Wolff/PhotoEdit (c) Quang Ho/Shutterstock.com (bl) LionH/E+/Getty Images (bc) DAVID BUFFINGTON/Media Bakery (br) beboy/ Shutterstock.com. 310 (tl) Lisa F. Young/ Shutterstock.com (tc) Canva Pty Ltd/Alamy Stock Photo (tr) Neil Juggins/Alamy Stock Photo (cl) Medioimages/Photodisc/Getty Images (cr) Ingram Publishing/Getty Images (bl) Andrei Radzkou/ Alamy Stock Photo (bc) Zeljko Radojko/ Shutterstock.com (br) Tetra Images/Getty Images.

Acknowledgments

The Authors and Publisher would like to thank the following reviewers and teaching professionals for their valuable feedback during the development of the series.

Literature Reviewers

Carmen Agra Deedy, Grace Lin, Jonda C. McNair, Anastasia Suen

Global Reviewers

USA:

Sandy Cano, Case Manager/Special Education Teacher, Pasteur Elementary School, Chicago, IL; **Sina Chau-Pech,** Elementary ELD Lead Teacher, Folsom Cordova Unified School District, Sacramento, CA; **Ana Sainz de la Peña,** Director, ESOL and Bilingual Programs, The School District of Philadelphia, Philadelphia Allentown, PA; **Griselda E. Flores,** Bilingual Instruction Coach, Chicago Public Schools, Chicago, IL; **Lisa King,** District Lead ESOL Teacher, Polo Road Elementary School, Columbia, SC; **Janie Oosterveen,** Bilingual Teacher Specialist, San Antonio Independent School District, San Antonio, TX; **Cristina Rojas, MS. Ed.,** District Program Specialist, EL Programs, Hacienda La Puente Unified School District, Hacienda Heights, CA; **Jennifer Skrocki Eargle,** District Elementary Language Arts Specialist & Contract Employee, Galena Park Independent School District, Houston, TX

Asia:

Mohan Aiyer, School Principal, Brainworks International School, Yangon; **Andrew Chuang,** Weige Primary School, Taipei; **Sherefa Dickson,** Head Teacher, SMIC, Beijing; **Ms Hien,** IP Manager, IPS Vietnam, Ho Chi Minh; **Christine Huang,** Principal, The International Bilingual School at the Hsinchu Science Park (IBSH), Hsinchu; **Julie Hwang,** Academic Consultant, Seoul; **David Kwok,** CEO, Englit Enterprise, Guangzhou; **Emily Li,** Teaching Assistant, SMIC, Beijing; **Warren Martin,** English Teacher, Houhai English, Beijing; **Bongse Memba,** Academic Coordinator, SMIC, Beijing; **Hoai Minh Nguyen,** Wellspring International Bilingual School, Ho Chi Minh; **Mark Robertson,** Elementary School Principal, Yangon Academy, Yangon; **Daphne Tseng,** American Eagle Institute, Hsinchu; **Amanda Xu,** Director of Teaching and Research, Englit Enterprise, Guangzhou; **Alice Yamamoto,** ALT, PL Gakuen Elementary School, Osaka; **Yan Yang,** Director of Research Development, Houhai English, Beijing

Middle East:

Lisa Olsen, Teacher, GEMS World Academy, Dubai, United Arab Emirates; **Erin Witthoft,** Curriculum Coordinator, Universal American School, Kuwait

Latin America:

Federico Brull, Academic Director, Cambridge School of Monterrey, Mexico; **Elizabeth Caballero,** English Coordinator, Ramiro Kolbe Campus Otay, Mexico; **Renata Callipo,** Teacher, CEI Romualdo, Brazil; **Lilia Huerta,** General Supervisor, Ramiro Kolbe Campus Presidentes, Mexico; **Rosalba Millán,** English Coordinator Primary, Instituto Cenca, Mexico; **Ann Marie Moreira,** Academic Consultant, Brazil; **Raúl Rivera,** English Coordinator, Ramiro Kolbe Campus Santa Fe, Mexico; **Leonardo Xavier,** Teacher, CEI Romualdo, Brazil

The Publisher gratefully acknowledges the contributions of the following National Geographic Explorers and photographers to our program and planet:

Maycira Costa, Elizabeth Kapu'uwailani Lindsey, Carsten Peter, and Constanza Ceruti